ANIMALS AND THEIR HABITATS

Oceans

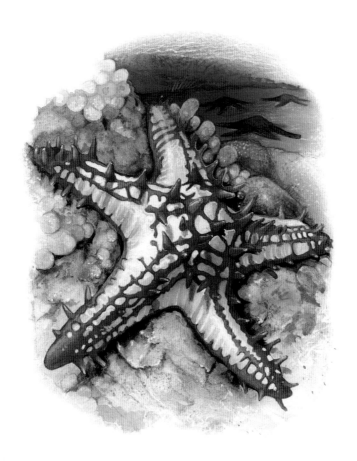

WORLD
BOOK

a Scott Fetzer company
Chicago
www.worldbook.com

For information about other World Book publications, visit our website at http://www.worldbook.com or call 1-800-WORLDBK (967-5325).

For information about sales to schools and libraries, call 1-800-975-3250 (United States), or 1-800-837-5365 (Canada).

2014 Revised Printing
© 2012 Amber Books Ltd., London.

Staff

Executive Committee
President: Donald D. Keller
Vice President and Editor in Chief: Paul A. Kobasa
Vice President, Sales & Marketing: Sean Lockwood
Vice President, International: Richard Flower
Controller: Yan Chen
Director, Human Resources: Bev Ecker

Editorial

Associate Director, Supplementary Publications:
  Scott Thomas
Managing Editor, Supplementary Publications:
  Barbara A. Mayes
Associate Manager, Supplementary Publications:
  Cassie Mayer
Editors: Brian Johnson and Kristina Vaicikonis
Researcher: Annie Brodsky
Editorial Assistant: Ethel Matthews
Manager, Contracts & Compliance
  (Rights & Permissions): Loranne K. Shields
Indexer: David Pofelski

Graphics and Design

Senior Manager: Tom Evans
Senior Designer: Don Di Sante
Manager, Cartography: Wayne K. Pichler
Senior Cartographer: John Rejba

Pre-Press and Manufacturing

Director: Carma Fazio
Manufacturing Manager: Steven K. Hueppchen
Senior Production Manager: Janice Rossing
Production/Technology Manager: Anne Fritzinger
Proofreader: Emilie Schrage

Product Development

Amber Books Ltd.
Writer: David Alderton
Project Editor: Sarah Uttridge
Designer: Andrew Easton
Editorial Assistant: Kieron Connolly

Library of Congress Cataloging-in-Publication Data

Oceans.
    p. cm. -- (Animals and their habitats)
    Summary: "Oceans cover just over 70% of the Earth's surface, and are home to hundreds of thousands of animals. This illustrated nonfiction volume introduces several ocean animals. Detailed captions describe each animal, while inset maps show where the animals can be found around the world. Features include a glossary, maps, photographs, and an index"-- Provided by publisher.
    Includes index.
    ISBN 978-0-7166-0447-1
    1. Marine animals--Juvenile literature. 2. Marine ecology-- Juvenile literature. I. World Book, Inc.
    QL122.2.O337 2012
    591.77--dc23
                                        2012005838

This printing:
ISBN: 978-0-7166-0539-3
Set ISBN: 978-0-7166-0533-1

Printed in China by Leo Paper Products, LTD., Heshan, Guangdong
2nd printing April 2014

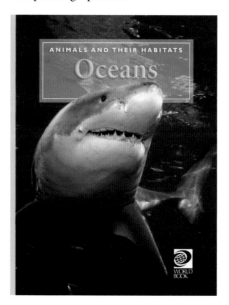

Cover image: The great white shark is a top predator among the many animal species that live in the world's oceans, which cover more than 70 percent of Earth's surface. Ocean animals range in size from microscopic one-celled organisms to the blue whale, the largest animal that has ever lived on Earth.

© SuperStock (Science Faction)

Contents

Introduction

Earth is a water planet. Oceans cover more than 70 percent of Earth's surface. The Pacific Ocean alone covers about one-third of Earth's surface. Near the equator, the Pacific stretches about 11,000 miles (17,700 kilometers) from Panama in the east to the Malay Peninsula in the west.

The oceans are also deep, averaging 13,000 feet (4,000 meters) from the surface to the sea floor. The deepest known spot is in the Mariana Trench in the western Pacific Ocean. This spot, called the Challenger Deep, lies 35,840 feet (10,924 meters) below sea level. If the world's highest mountain were placed in the Challenger Deep, it would be covered by more than 1.3 miles (2.1 kilometers) of water.

If there were no oceans, life as we know it could not exist. Most scientists believe that life first appeared in the oceans. Today, the oceans are home to hundreds of thousands of different *species* (kinds) of living things. Some species make their own food, using the energy in sunlight. Others are predators, which feed on other living things.

The oceans are home to many fearsome predators. One of the most powerful is the great white shark. It has sharp, triangular teeth with jagged edges. Its powerful jaws can rip chunks of flesh from seals and sea lions, two of its favorite prey.

COMMON OCTOPUS

Ocean animals have developed many remarkable *adaptations* (characteristics) to escape from predators. For example, an octopus can confuse a predator by squirting a cloud of ink, allowing it to speed away using jet propulsion. A cuttlefish can rapidly change the color of its skin. These color changes may startle a predator or enable the cuttlefish to blend in with its surroundings.

There are many different habitats in the oceans. A habitat is the kind of place in which a plant or animal lives. The richest habitats in the oceans are coral reefs. Coral reefs look like

WHALE SHARK

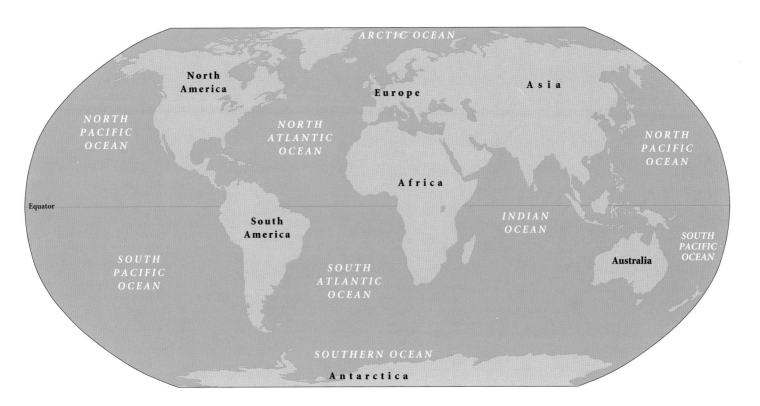

OCEANS

colorful, underwater gardens, but they are actually made up of animals called corals. These animals spend their entire adult lives in one place, gradually building skeletons made of limestone. A tremendous variety of fish and other animals live on coral reefs. The reefs provide many places for animals to hide from hungry predators. But predators such as the ferocious moray eel also hide away on the reef, ambushing prey that ventures too close.

Other ocean habitats are harsh, such as the bitterly cold waters of the Arctic Ocean. Still, this habitat teems with life. Tiny shrimplike creatures live beneath the ice. Shellfish live on the sandy sea floor. Seals hunt from the sea ice, protected from the cold by a thick layer of fat beneath their skin.

The harshest habitat of all may be the ocean depths. But even here, scientists have found a huge variety of life. People have hardly begun to explore the depths of the oceans. In fact, we know more about the surface of the moon than we do about the deep ocean.

COMMON SEAL

Great Hammerhead Shark

VITAL STATISTICS

WEIGHT	507–992 lb (230–450 kg); pregnant females can weigh 1,278 lb (580 kg)
LENGTH	Females up to 18 ft (5.5 m); males up to 11 ft (3.4 m)
SEXUAL MATURITY	Females at 6.8 ft (2.1 m) and 90 lb (41 kg); males at 7.4 ft (2.25 m) and 112 lb (51 kg)
INCUBATION PERIOD	About 10 months
NUMBER OF OFFSPRING	Up to 55, measuring 28 in (70 cm)
DIET	Rays, smaller sharks, squid, and bony fish
LIFE SPAN	20–30 years

There are several species of hammerhead sharks. The great hammerheads are the largest. Like many other sharks, hammerheads have become endangered because of overfishing.

WHERE IN THE WORLD?

Found throughout tropical oceans worldwide, usually close to reefs, sometimes even swimming in shallow water close to the coast.

ANIMAL FACTS

The wide, flat head provides extra space for sense organs the shark uses to track prey. The animal has a keen sense of smell and can quickly trace the source of blood in the water. Special organs also detect electrical signals given off by prey hidden on the sea floor. The shark's head also helps it to turn quickly. The great hammerhead is usually not dangerous to people unless provoked.

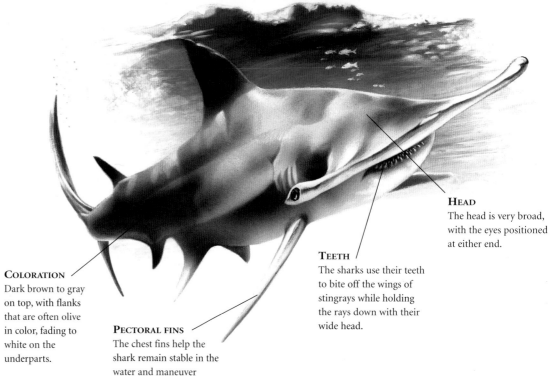

COLORATION
Dark brown to gray on top, with flanks that are often olive in color, fading to white on the underparts.

PECTORAL FINS
The chest fins help the shark remain stable in the water and maneuver easily.

TEETH
The sharks use their teeth to bite off the wings of stingrays while holding the rays down with their wide head.

HEAD
The head is very broad, with the eyes positioned at either end.

FISHING STRATEGY
Swimming over the sea floor disturbs the sand, flushing out any rays hiding there so the hammerhead can catch them.

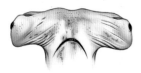

The head, seen from below, with one eye and one nostril at either end

HOW BIG IS IT?

Great White Shark

The most feared of all sharks, the great white is a powerful *predator* (hunting animal). Despite their reputation, great white sharks rarely bite people, and most attacks appear to be accidental.

VITAL STATISTICS

WEIGHT	5,000–7,000 lb (2,250–3,180 kg)
LENGTH	18–21 ft (5.5–6.5 m)
SEXUAL MATURITY	Females from 13 ft (4 m) long, typically at 12–14 years; males from 11.5 ft (3.5 m), 9–10 years
INCUBATION PERIOD	1 year
NUMBER OF OFFSPRING	8–9, but can be up to 14
DIET	Hunts rays, sharks, dolphins, squid, and bony fish; favors seals in many areas
LIFE SPAN	40–60 years, possibly longer

WHERE IN THE WORLD?

Roams throughout the oceans but is often found in coastal waters. Common around Australia and South Africa, as well as off the California coast.

ANIMAL FACTS

The great white shark is warm-blooded, unlike most other fish. This feature enables it to strike quickly even in cold waters. The female protects the eggs inside her body until they hatch. Great white sharks that attack people appear to have mistaken them for seals. However, bites are so rare that people are far likelier to die from lightning strikes. The numbers of these sharks appear to be falling quickly, largely because of illegal fishing.

Great whites have extremely powerful jaws.

HEAD
The head is cone-shaped. The mouth, which is on the underside, contains about 3,000 teeth.

COLORATION
Upperparts are gray, sometimes with a blue or brownish hue. Only the underparts are white.

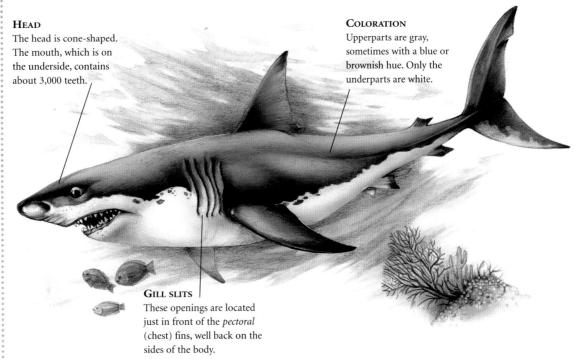

GILL SLITS
These openings are located just in front of the *pectoral* (chest) fins, well back on the sides of the body.

REPLACEMENT TEETH

Great whites have up to five rows of teeth. When a tooth in the front row breaks or is lost, a tooth from the second row moves forward to replace it. The teeth in the other rows also move forward, and a new tooth forms in the last row.

HOW BIG IS IT?

RIPPING PREY APART
The great white shark's serrated teeth saw through flesh as it shakes its head from side to side, cutting off chunks.

Whale Shark

VITAL STATISTICS

WEIGHT	Average 20 tons (18.7 metric tons)
LENGTH	18–40 ft (5.5–12.2 m)
SEXUAL MATURITY	Females may not breed until they are 30 years old
INCUBATION PERIOD	Eggs develop in the female's body and hatch before live birth
NUMBER OF OFFSPRING	300 pups recorded in 1 female; no parental care
DIET	Filters plankton from the water
LIFE SPAN	Up to 100 years

Whale sharks are not only the largest sharks but also the largest fish in the oceans. However, they do not reach the size of true whales. Whale sharks feed by filtering the water for tiny animals.

WHERE IN THE WORLD?

Found in tropical and warmer areas in the world's oceans, often near the shore. Seasonal gatherings of these sharks occur in some areas.

ANIMAL FACTS

The whale shark's mouth measures about 5 feet (1.5 meters) wide, allowing it to filter large volumes of water for *plankton* (tiny drifting organisms). The plankton are filtered out by the gills and then swallowed directly. Water exits the body through the gill flaps. The animal has more than 300 rows of small teeth whose function is unknown. Whale sharks are not fast swimmers, usually traveling at just 3 miles (5 kilometers) per hour. Scientists believe that the whale shark's numbers are falling from overfishing.

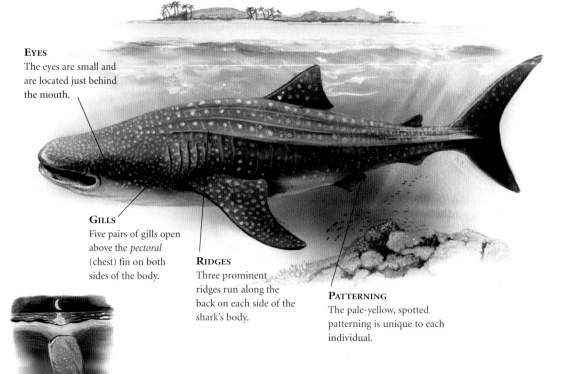

EYES
The eyes are small and are located just behind the mouth.

GILLS
Five pairs of gills open above the *pectoral* (chest) fin on both sides of the body.

RIDGES
Three prominent ridges run along the back on each side of the shark's body.

PATTERNING
The pale-yellow, spotted patterning is unique to each individual.

FEEDING MOVEMENTS
Whale sharks feed near the surface on the great numbers of plankton that move up from the ocean depths at night.

TRAVELING COMPANIONS

Whale sharks are often accompanied by small cleaner fish, which keep the bodies of these giants free from parasites.

The flattened profile of the whale shark reduces water resistance, so it can swim more easily.

HOW BIG IS IT?

Devil Ray

VITAL STATISTICS

WEIGHT	About 770 lb (350 kg)
LENGTH	Up to 17 ft (520 m)
SEXUAL MATURITY	Possibly not reached until 20–30 years
INCUBATION PERIOD	Uncertain— could be up to 25 months
NUMBER OF OFFSPRING	1; weighs 77 lb (35 kg) at birth
DIET	Filters the water for *plankton* (tiny organisms)
LIFE SPAN	Probably 70 years or more

ANIMAL FACTS

Like sharks, rays have a skeleton made of *cartilage* (rubbery tissue) rather than bone. Female devil rays produce live offspring, with the eggs developing and hatching in their bodies. A young ray is actually rolled up during its growth in its mother's body and unfurls its wings only after it is born. Despite their size and stinging tail, these rays fall victim to various sharks. But the main threat to devil rays is overfishing by people. Scientists are not certain how many devil rays remain, but they worry that numbers of the fish are falling.

Devil rays are often accompanied by smaller fish called remoras, which cling to their bodies, helping to remove any parasites.

Devil rays are closely related to sharks. They feed on tiny ocean animals that drift with the currents. The tail contains a stinger that the devil ray uses to defend itself from *predators* (hunting animals).

WHERE IN THE WORLD?

Swims throughout the warmer areas of the oceans, from east Africa through the Pacific to the western coasts of the Americas. Also found in the Atlantic.

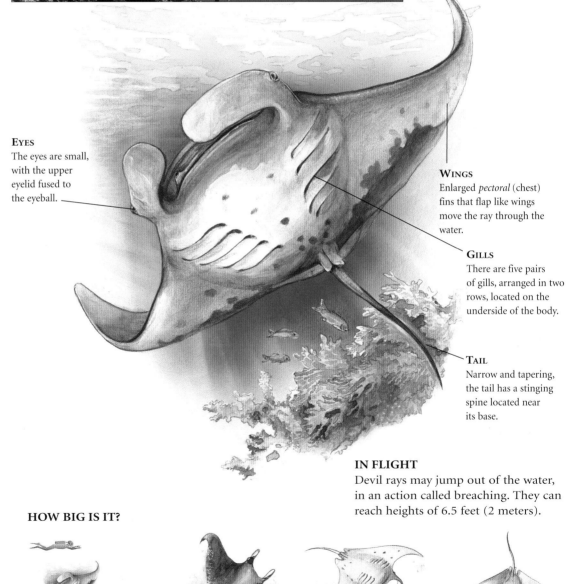

EYES
The eyes are small, with the upper eyelid fused to the eyeball.

WINGS
Enlarged *pectoral* (chest) fins that flap like wings move the ray through the water.

GILLS
There are five pairs of gills, arranged in two rows, located on the underside of the body.

TAIL
Narrow and tapering, the tail has a stinging spine located near its base.

IN FLIGHT
Devil rays may jump out of the water, in an action called breaching. They can reach heights of 6.5 feet (2 meters).

HOW BIG IS IT?

Yellowfin Tuna

VITAL STATISTICS

WEIGHT	Up to 440 lb (200 kg)
LENGTH	Up to 7.9 ft (2.4 m)
SEXUAL MATURITY	1.6–2 years
NUMBER OF EGGS	Up to 3 million annually; spawning occurs almost year-round
HATCHING PERIOD	1 day; *larvae* (immature forms) drift in the plankton
DIET	Small fish, shrimp, and squids
LIFE SPAN	15–30 years

ANIMAL FACTS

The flesh of these tuna fish is reddish because it has high levels of a chemical rich in iron and oxygen. An abundance of oxygen enables the fish to swim at great speeds, giving them an advantage over prey. Their flesh is especially prized in sushi. Yellowfins are not as valuable as bluefin tunas, which are in danger of extinction in the Atlantic Ocean. In some areas, yellowfins often swim near dolphins. This may protect them from sharks, which are their main *predator* (hunting animal). Sharks are reluctant to approach dolphins, which are known to attack them. However, this has led to the deaths of many dolphins, which may become trapped in fishing nets with the tuna. Yellowfin tuna are now farmed in some areas.

These remarkable fish are perfectly adapted to slicing through the water at high speed. They have become a popular food fish, especially in sushi.

WHERE IN THE WORLD?

Lives in tropical and warm waters on both sides of the equator. Not present in the Mediterranean Sea.

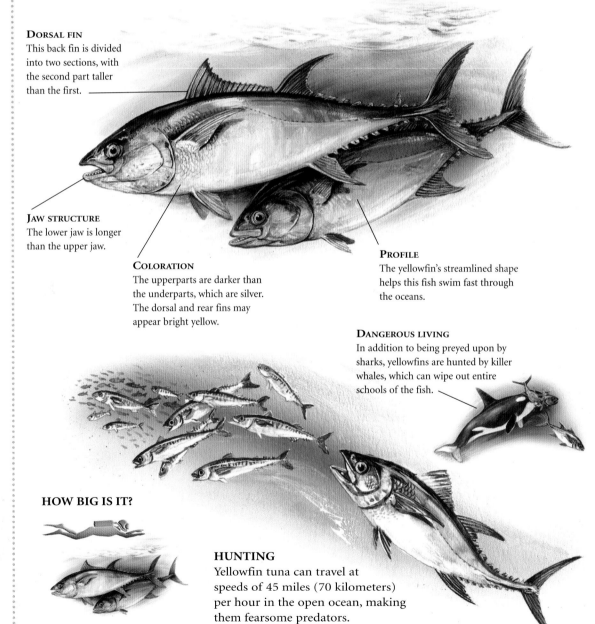

DORSAL FIN
This back fin is divided into two sections, with the second part taller than the first.

JAW STRUCTURE
The lower jaw is longer than the upper jaw.

COLORATION
The upperparts are darker than the underparts, which are silver. The dorsal and rear fins may appear bright yellow.

PROFILE
The yellowfin's streamlined shape helps this fish swim fast through the oceans.

DANGEROUS LIVING
In addition to being preyed upon by sharks, yellowfins are hunted by killer whales, which can wipe out entire schools of the fish.

HOW BIG IS IT?

HUNTING
Yellowfin tuna can travel at speeds of 45 miles (70 kilometers) per hour in the open ocean, making them fearsome predators.

Bluefaced Angelfish

Angelfish are among the most colorful of creatures that live on tropical coral reefs. They are solitary by nature. Their appearance changes dramatically as they mature.

VITAL STATISTICS

WEIGHT	2.4 lb (1.1 kg)
LENGTH	15 in (38 cm)
SEXUAL MATURITY	1 year; females can transform into males
NUMBER OF EGGS	25,000–75,000 tiny, floating eggs that drift with the plankton
HATCHING PERIOD	1 day; young stop drifting by 4 weeks, after feeding on *plankton* (tiny organisms)
DIET	Feeds on sponges and algae, among other foods
LIFE SPAN	5–12 years

WHERE IN THE WORLD?

Found in the Indo-Pacific, from East Africa and the Maldives east to Vanuatu and north to the Yaeyama Islands. Also present around Palau and Krosae in Micronesia.

ANIMAL FACTS

The bluefaced angelfish is one of the largest *species* (kinds) of angelfish. It roams reefs in search of food. It is often observed in gulleys and near caves. Young fish are relatively hard to spot because they hide in shallow caves, preferably ones near patches of algae, one of their main foods. When spawning, bluefaced angelfish form pairs, depending on the number of fish in the area. However, where they are more numerous, spawning takes place in groups. There is no way to tell the sexes apart by sight.

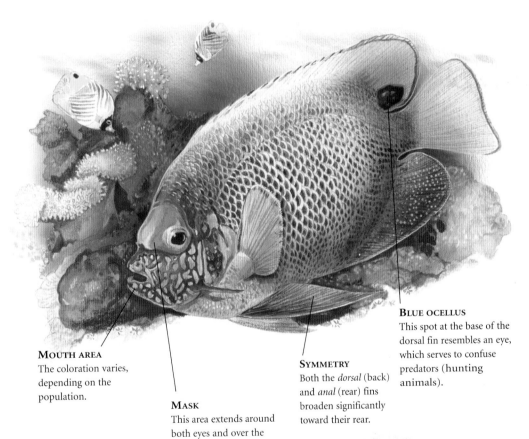

MOUTH AREA
The coloration varies, depending on the population.

MASK
This area extends around both eyes and over the forehead.

SYMMETRY
Both the *dorsal* (back) and *anal* (rear) fins broaden significantly toward their rear.

BLUE OCELLUS
This spot at the base of the dorsal fin resembles an eye, which serves to confuse predators (hunting animals).

Most young angelfish are blue with stripes or concentric patterning on their bodies.

HOW BIG IS IT?

STAYING SAFE

Angelfish use retreats on the reef where they can hide from such predators as sharks. They defend these retreats from other fish.

Queen Parrotfish

VITAL STATISTICS

LENGTH	6–48 in (15–122 cm); "supermales" reach double this length
NUMBER OF EGGS	Several thousand
HATCHING PERIOD	1 day; *larvae* (immature forms) drift and do not feed for 3 days
HABITAT	Tropical coral reefs
DIET	Algae on corals and rocks; also sponges
LIFE SPAN	Up to 5 years

ANIMAL FACTS

The powerful jaws of queen parrotfish crunch up the limestone skeletons of coral, which they pass from their body as fine sand. At dusk, they produce a cocoon of mucus, in which they spend the night. The cocoon protects them from *predators* (hunting animals) by masking their scent. Queen parrotfish have both male and female reproductive organs when they hatch. Some of the fish develop into males and others into females. But some become "supermales." These males are larger than other parrotfish. Supermales usually breed with three or four females.

The shape of the parrotfish's mouthparts helps it to obtain its food.

Parrotfish are large and spectacular residents of the coral reef. Their name refers to their dazzling coloration. Unfortunately, they damage corals to get at the algae that live inside.

WHERE IN THE WORLD?

This species lives in the western Atlantic, ranging from Bermuda to Florida and the Bahamas in the north to the area around northern South America in the south.

PEDICELLARIAE
Located at the base of the spines, these clawlike structures prevent the body from becoming overgrown with algae.

CAUDAL FIN
This rear fin is broad, with "points" on the top and bottom.

COLORATION
Coloration can be individual, with the brightly colored eye linked with the head markings.

HARMFUL HABITS
Unfortunately, these colorful fish destroy coral to get at the algae that live inside.

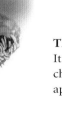

SCALES
The scales covering the body are relatively large and easy to see.

BEAK
The stout mouthparts are used to scrape up algae.

HOW BIG IS IT?

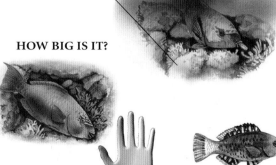

TRANSFORMATION

It is not just the parrotfish's sex that may change as it matures. Its coloration and appearance may also change.

Common Clownfish

These fish are also called anemonefish because of their remarkable partnership with sea anemones. The fish have become rare in some areas because so many have been taken for aquariums.

VITAL STATISTICS

LENGTH	Up to 4.3 in (11 cm); females are larger
SEXUAL MATURITY	1–1.5 years
NUMBER OF EGGS	100–10,000, depending on female's age
HATCHING PERIOD	About 7 days, depending on water temperature; the young drift with the currents for up to 12 days
HABITAT	Shallow, calm areas of reef, with host anemones
LIFE SPAN	6–10 years in the wild; 12 in an aquarium

WHERE IN THE WORLD?

Lives in the eastern Indian Ocean, from Thailand and Malaysia to northwestern Australia, and north via the Philippines, Taiwan, and Japan to the Ryukyu Islands.

ANIMAL FACTS

Clownfish live among the stinging tentacles of sea anemones, where *predators* (hunting animals) cannot follow. A special mucus protects the fish from being stung. In return, the clownfish rid anemones of debris and parasites. They also attack fish that might try to feed on the anemones. Clownfish scare away predators with pulses of sound made by slamming their teeth together. Clownfish often live in small groups, with a breeding male and female and several smaller, non-breeding males. If the female dies, the breeding male becomes female. The next-largest fish then becomes the breeding male.

The *dorsal* (back) fin is divided into two parts, with protective spines at the front.

FIN SHAPE
The fins are generally rounded, with relatively large *pectoral* (chest) fins.

TAIL
The tail is short and the fins are edged in black.

PATTERNING
Although clownfish look similar, their patterning is different enough to tell them apart.

BREEDING BEHAVIOR
A breeding female usually *spawns* (releases eggs) very near to its host anemone, after the breeding pair cleans an area for the eggs.

HOW BIG IS IT?

Devil Lionfish

VITAL STATISTICS

WEIGHT	2.5 lb (1.1 kg)
LENGTH	Up to 15 in (38 cm)
SEXUAL MATURITY	2 years
NUMBER OF EGGS	2,000–15,000 laid in balls, which are fertilized externally
HATCHING PERIOD	*Larvae* (immature forms) spend 25–40 days drifting with the currents before falling to the reef
DIET	Hunts small fish, shrimp, and crabs
LIFE SPAN	10–15 years

ANIMAL FACTS

Devil lionfish live on coral reefs in relatively shallow coastal waters. Their coloration provides camouflage, helping them to blend in against the background of the reef. They swim slowly and can look like drifting seaweed. They are also protected from *predators* (hunting animals) by their venomous spines, which can kill other fish and cause intense pain for people. Unfortunately, lionfish have escaped into the Caribbean Sea, probably because people released them from home aquariums. Lionfish have devastated wildlife on coral reefs in the region. Native fish have few defenses against the lionfish, which faces no predators. A single lionfish can eat about 80 percent of the small fish on a small coral reef in only a few weeks.

This beautiful reef fish is also known as the zebrafish, turkeyfish, lionfish, or firefish. These common names refer to the fish's coloration, its "mane" of fins and spines, and its fiery, painful *venom* (poison).

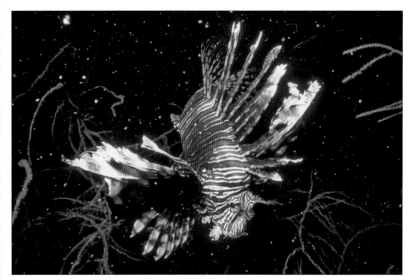

WHERE IN THE WORLD?

Lives in the Red Sea south to the waters of South Africa and east across the Indian Ocean. Also in the eastern Mediterranean. Introduced to the Caribbean Sea by people.

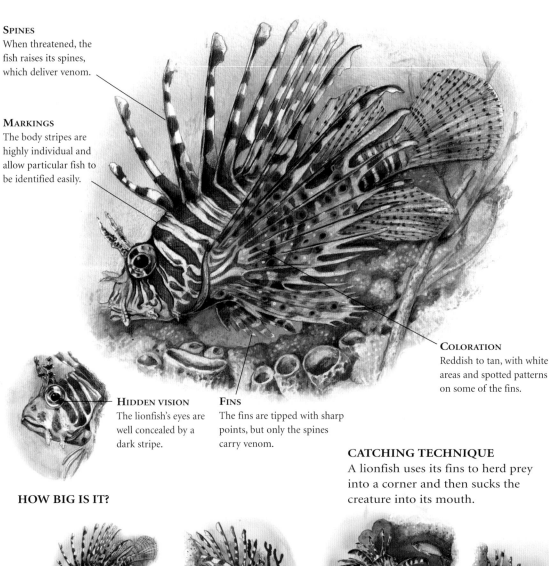

SPINES
When threatened, the fish raises its spines, which deliver venom.

MARKINGS
The body stripes are highly individual and allow particular fish to be identified easily.

HIDDEN VISION
The lionfish's eyes are well concealed by a dark stripe.

FINS
The fins are tipped with sharp points, but only the spines carry venom.

COLORATION
Reddish to tan, with white areas and spotted patterns on some of the fins.

HOW BIG IS IT?

CATCHING TECHNIQUE
A lionfish uses its fins to herd prey into a corner and then sucks the creature into its mouth.

Spiny Porcupinefish

These bizarre fish also may be called longspined porcupinefish, spiny puffers, or balloonfish. These names refer to the fish's protective spines and the way it can inflate its body when threatened.

VITAL STATISTICS

HABITAT	Coral reefs, at depths of 6–328 ft (2–100 m)
LENGTH	8–15 in (20–36 cm), up to 20 in (50 cm)
SEXUAL MATURITY	Around 9 months
HATCHING PERIOD	About 4 days; *larvae* (immature forms) drift with the currents and change into a mature form in 3 weeks
SPAWNING	Occurs at the water surface, where the round eggs float
DIET	Sea urchins, hermit crabs, snails
LIFE SPAN	5–7 years

ANIMAL FACTS

A spiny porcupinefish can transform its shape when threatened. By inflating its stomach with water or air, the fish can make itself difficult to swallow, especially as its spines rise. The fish's powerful teeth provide a second line of defense, as they can inflict a painful bite. Close relatives of these fish are highly *venomous* (poisonous), but the spines of this species contain little if any venom. Adults are solitary, but the young often associate in groups.

These fish can inflate themselves with air for protection from hungry birds at the surface.

WHERE IN THE WORLD?

Ranges from Florida to Brazil, around South Africa to the Indian Ocean. Found throughout the Pacific, but especially common in the west and Oceania.

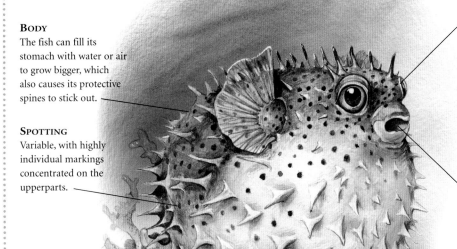

BODY
The fish can fill its stomach with water or air to grow bigger, which also causes its protective spines to stick out.

SPOTTING
Variable, with highly individual markings concentrated on the upperparts.

EYES
These are large and help the fish to spot *predators* (hunting animals) quickly. Porcupinefish are not strong swimmers, so they must inflate to escape.

MOUTHPARTS
The fish have two large teeth, one upper and one lower, that stick out like a beak.

FEEDING POWER
Strong teeth enable them to break apart hard-shelled *invertebrates* (animals without backbones). They tend to hunt at night.

DIFFERENT PERSPECTIVE
Spiny porcupinefish may not be able to outswim predators, but their ability to grow larger gives them a powerful defense.

HOW BIG IS IT?

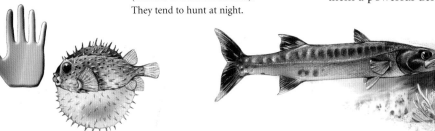

Seahorse

The head of this unusual fish resembles that of a horse, which explains its common name. Seahorses are wonderfully camouflaged to blend in with ocean vegetation.

VITAL STATISTICS

LENGTH	0.6–10 in (1.6–25 cm)
SEXUAL MATURITY	4 months– 1 year
NUMBER OF EGGS	Average 100– 200
INCUBATION PERIOD	14–28 days; one day after the young leave the pouch, the adult pair mates again
HABITAT	Areas of sea grass, mangrove forests, and coral reefs
DIET	Tiny shrimp and other *invertebrates* (animals without backbones)
LIFE SPAN	1–5 years

ANIMAL FACTS

Seahorses are well camouflaged to blend in with ocean vegetation. Some look remarkably like seaweed. By holding on to a stalk of seaweed with its tail, the seahorse can sway with the currents, just as the seaweed does. Although seahorses often live near tropical reefs, they are also found in a variety of mild coastal waters. Pairs bond for the length of the breeding season. Unusually, the male provides parental care, protecting the eggs in a belly pouch.

Seahorses are covered with projections that help them to resemble seaweed.

WHERE IN THE WORLD?

Lives in relatively warm coastal waters, mangrove forests, and coral reefs. Most common in the western Atlantic Ocean and the Indo-Pacific region.

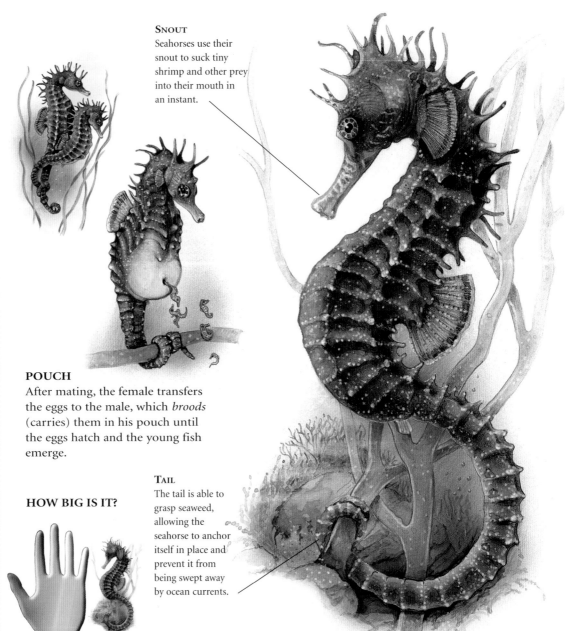

SNOUT
Seahorses use their snout to suck tiny shrimp and other prey into their mouth in an instant.

POUCH
After mating, the female transfers the eggs to the male, which *broods* (carries) them in his pouch until the eggs hatch and the young fish emerge.

HOW BIG IS IT?

TAIL
The tail is able to grasp seaweed, allowing the seahorse to anchor itself in place and prevent it from being swept away by ocean currents.

Mediterranean Moray Eel

VITAL STATISTICS

WEIGHT	Typically about 33 lb (15 kg)
LENGTH	Up to about 5 ft (1.5 meters)
SEXUAL MATURITY	Probably about 5 years
HATCHING PERIOD	A few days, depending on water temperature
NUMBER OF EGGS	60,000, laid in open water, from which tiny, transparent *larvae* (immature forms) hatch
DIET	Fish, crabs, and squid; may also scavenge
LIFE SPAN	Up to 20 years

Although these fearsome eels look a bit like snakes, they are actually fish. Their narrow body enables them to hide in rocky *burrows* (shelters) and other small spaces from which they can lunge at prey.

WHERE IN THE WORLD?

Moray eels live in the world's tropical and warmer waters, typically on coral reefs.

ANIMAL FACTS

Moray eels must feed on relatively small animals because they have such narrow jaws. They hunt largely by their sense of smell, as they have small eyes and poor eyesight. They typically hide during the day and come out at night to hunt. Moray eels are unusual in having a set of secondary jaws at the back of the mouth. These jaws spring forward and help the eel to hold and swallow prey. There are many different *species* (kinds) of moray eel.

TEETH
Strong, backward-pointing teeth allow the eel to rip flesh.

MOUTH
Powerful jaws help to seize prey. The eel also has a second set of toothed jaws that it uses to drag prey into its throat.

APPEARANCE
The sleek, scaleless skin is covered by a thick layer of protective mucus.

FINS
The *dorsal* (back) fin starts just behind the head and runs down the middle of the back.

The moray eel's patterning helps it to hide.

HOW BIG IS IT?

SMALL AND BRIGHT

Ribbon eels are perhaps the most beautiful morays. Found in Asian waters, they are black at first but change color as they grow. Males become blue and females become yellow.

Fiddler Crab

VITAL STATISTICS

LENGTH	Up to 2 in (5 cm); the male's claw is of similar length
NUMBER OF EGGS	850–1,600; the female remains in a burrow for 2 weeks while carrying the eggs
INCUBATION PERIOD	*Larvae* (immature forms) hatch after 12–14 days
HABITAT	Beaches, mud flats, mangrove forests
DIET	Scrapes algae from grains of sand picked up in balls
LIFE SPAN	2–3 years

ANIMAL FACTS

Fiddler crabs use their small claws and mouthparts to sift through sand for tiny food particles. The sand forms little balls that the crab leaves behind. As a result, a fiddler crab's *burrow* (shelter) may be surrounded by many little balls of sand. After fiddler crabs mate, the eggs develop under the female's body. When the eggs are ready to hatch, she heads back to the sea. The young are tiny, free-swimming *larvae* (immature forms) that hardly resemble adult crabs. To grow, they *molt* (shed) their tough *exoskeleton* (external skeleton) to grow a larger one. They molt several times. Eventually, the young look like miniature crabs and return to the shore.

Male fiddler crabs wave their large claw to threaten other males or to attract females. This motion somewhat resembles the movements of a person playing a fiddle.

WHERE IN THE WORLD?

Ranges widely in warmer climates, living on the Pacific and Atlantic coasts of the Americas as well as in the Indian Ocean.

EYES
The eyes are raised on stalks, giving the crab a better view of its surroundings.

CARAPACE
This tough casing covers their upper body.

CLAW
Only the male develops a massive claw. But it cannot use the claw for feeding, because the claw is too large to maneuver to its mouth.

LIMBS
Like all crabs, fiddler crabs have five pairs of legs. They walk on the back four pairs and use the front pair like hands.

PUTTING ON THE SQUEEZE
Male fiddler crabs use their large, powerful claws to wrestle with each other.

HOW BIG IS IT?

CLAW WAVING
A male waves his large claw to attract females. The size of the claw helps to signal how healthy the male is. Each species has its own style of waving.

Hermit Crab

VITAL STATISTICS

LENGTH	1-3 in (2.5–7.6 cm)
NUMBER OF EGGS	200–7,000
INCUBATION PERIOD	*Larvae* (immature forms) hatch after 2–3 weeks, once the female releases her eggs into the sea
HABITAT	In the sea and on land, though land species are vulnerable to drying out
DIET	Scavenges on animal and plant remains
LIFE SPAN	Up to 10 years; can be 20 in captivity

ANIMAL FACTS

There are hundreds of *species* (kinds) of hermit crabs. They tend to live in *colonies* (groups). The crabs use their shell to protect their soft abdomens, which they twist into the shell. The walking legs and claws are covered with a hard, thick material called chitin. They usually remain outside the shell. The crabs must exchange their shell for a larger one as they grow. They sometimes fight over shells, especially in areas where shells are scarce. Crabs will even steal the shells of living snails. A small number of hermit crabs do not live in shells. They tend to hide in holes in coral or rock.

A hermit crab larva

Hermit crabs do not grow the shells they carry. Instead, they occupy shells that they find in their environment. Most hermit crabs use shells made by snails.

WHERE IN THE WORLD?

Lives mainly in coastal areas, throughout tropical and warm waters of the world's oceans.

SHELL
This protects the crab's vulnerable abdomen. In some cases, the crab can withdraw its entire body into the shell for protection.

COLORATION
Although some hermit crabs are bright red, their color is often dull.

EYES
Set high, these work with the antennae, enabling the crab to survey its surroundings.

LEGS
Tapering to points and curving backward, the legs carry the crab and its shell.

HOLDING ON
Hermit crabs have claspers on the abdomen, which anchor the crab to its shell.

HOW BIG IS IT?

PREDATORS
Cuttlefish and octopuses can use their strong arms to pull hermit crabs out of their shells. Other *predators* (hunting animals) can suck the crabs out of their shells.

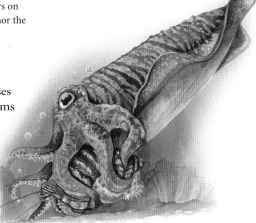
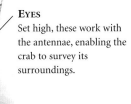

American Lobster

SPECIES · *Homarus americanus*

VITAL STATISTICS

WEIGHT	Typically 1.1–8.8 lb (0.5–4 kg); can reach over 44 lb (20 kg)
LENGTH	8–24 in (20–60 cm) but may grow to over 3.2 ft (1 m)
NUMBER OF EGGS	4,000–75,000 or more, depending on size
INCUBATION PERIOD	Eggs are carried by the female for 9–11 months
DIET	Mostly scavenges on animal remains but also eats small fish and other ocean creatures
LIFE SPAN	Can live over 100 years in the wild

ANIMAL FACTS

Hundreds of *species* (kinds) are known as lobsters but not all of them are closely related. American lobsters have poor eyesight because they live on the gloomy sea floor. They rely mainly on their antennae to sense their surroundings. Unlike the blood of most animals, a lobster's blood is blue because it is rich in copper. Mothers carry their eggs on the underside of the tail for about 10 months, until they hatch. Only one in a thousand of the offspring will still be alive a month later.

Young lobsters are especially vulnerable to predators.

American lobsters are prized for the meat in their claws and tails. However, until the 1800's, lobsters were held in such low regard that farmers ground them up to use as fertilizer.

WHERE IN THE WORLD?

Found along the Atlantic Coast of North America, from Labrador south to North Carolina.

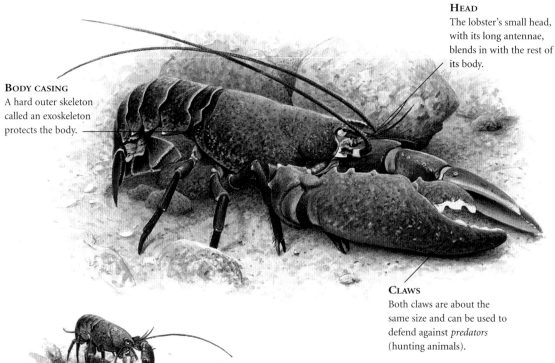

HEAD
The lobster's small head, with its long antennae, blends in with the rest of its body.

BODY CASING
A hard outer skeleton called an exoskeleton protects the body.

CLAWS
Both claws are about the same size and can be used to defend against *predators* (hunting animals).

ON THE MOVE
Lobsters normally walk over the seabed, but they can swim from danger by using their tail to propel themselves backward.

HOW BIG IS IT?

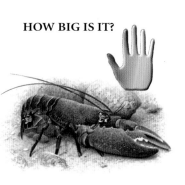

HUNTING PREY
Lobsters ambush their prey, using their powerful claws to seize passing fish.

Cleaner Shrimp

VITAL STATISTICS

LENGTH	1.25–1.5 in (3–4 cm)
SEXUAL MATURITY	1–2 months
NUMBER OF EGGS	Up to 1,000, produced every 1–2 weeks, carried under the female's abdomen
INCUBATION PERIOD	*Larvae* (immature forms) hatch at 12–14 days, emerging at night
HABITAT	Coral reefs in warmer waters around the world
DIET	Feeds on tiny ocean animals
LIFE SPAN	4–12 months

ANIMAL FACTS

Cleaner shrimp feed on *parasites*—a type of animal that feeds off another living thing, called a *host*. These parasites live on the bodies of their hosts, weakening them. There are special areas on a reef, described as "cleaner stations," where these shrimp gather and fish line up to be cleaned of parasites, dead skin, algae, and other unwanted material. The fish swim in particular patterns that signal to the shrimp that they are in no danger of being eaten. This applies even if the fish would normally feed on the shrimp.

A close-up of the shrimp's head shows the segmented feelers, called antennae.

In a remarkable alliance, cleaner shrimp eat harmful animals that live on the bodies of fish and other ocean creatures. The shrimp gain a steady supply of food, and the fish are freed of pests.

WHERE IN THE WORLD?

Found on tropical coral reefs around much of the world.

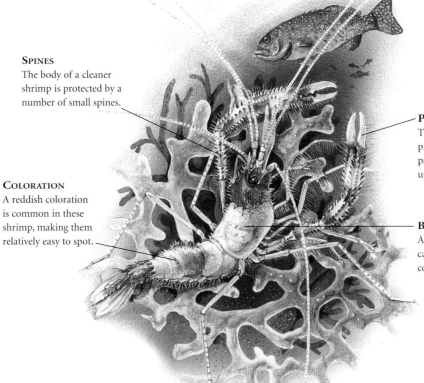

SPINES
The body of a cleaner shrimp is protected by a number of small spines.

COLORATION
A reddish coloration is common in these shrimp, making them relatively easy to spot.

PINCERS
These help the shrimp to probe effectively, remove parasites from fish, and pick up edible items.

BODY COVERING
A hard external casing, called an exoskeleton, covers the body.

HOW BIG IS IT?

MUTUALISM
The mutually beneficial relationship between fish and cleaner shrimp is called mutualism. It is one form of *symbiosis* (a relationship between two creatures in which at least one of them benefits).

Common Octopus

VITAL STATISTICS

WEIGHT	6.6–15 lb (3–6 kg)
LENGTH	Mantle can be 10 in (25 cm); legs up to 3.3 ft (1 m)
SEXUAL MATURITY	1–2 years
HATCHING PERIOD	Eggs hatch after about 1 month
NUMBER OF OFFSPRING	Females lay 100,000–500,000 eggs, which they guard until hatched; the females die soon afterward
DIET	Shellfish, including lobsters, which may be stolen from traps, and fish
LIFE SPAN	1–2 years

Octopuses are considered the most intelligent of all *invertebrates* (animals without backbones). They are able to solve problems and learn from past experiences. They even play with toys.

WHERE IN THE WORLD?

Range from the English Channel south through the Mediterranean, to the coast of West Africa and west via Cape Verde and the Canary Islands to the Azores.

ANIMAL FACTS

Few creatures are better masters of camouflage than octopuses. These relatives of cuttlefish and squid are able to change the color of their skin to blend in with their surroundings. If threatened, they can produce a cloud of purplish-black ink, squirted in the direction of a *predator* (hunting animal). This gives them the opportunity to escape. Octopuses live in dens, where they may store shellfish to ensure they have enough food. They are able to open shells with their powerful arms.

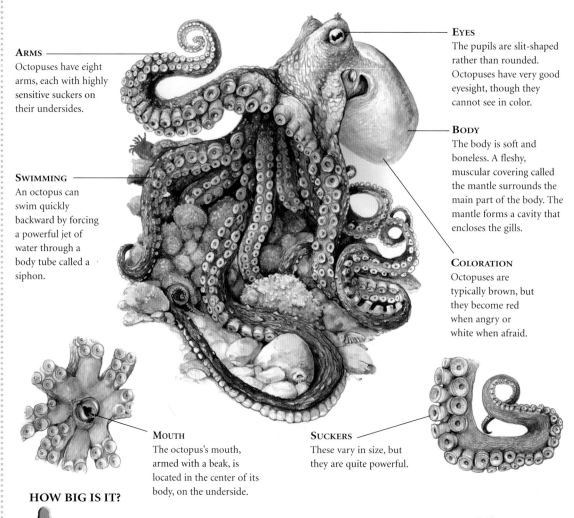

ARMS
Octopuses have eight arms, each with highly sensitive suckers on their undersides.

SWIMMING
An octopus can swim quickly backward by forcing a powerful jet of water through a body tube called a siphon.

EYES
The pupils are slit-shaped rather than rounded. Octopuses have very good eyesight, though they cannot see in color.

BODY
The body is soft and boneless. A fleshy, muscular covering called the mantle surrounds the main part of the body. The mantle forms a cavity that encloses the gills.

COLORATION
Octopuses are typically brown, but they become red when angry or white when afraid.

MOUTH
The octopus's mouth, armed with a beak, is located in the center of its body, on the underside.

SUCKERS
These vary in size, but they are quite powerful.

HOW BIG IS IT?

EGGS
The female octopus lays her eggs in rocky crevices.

Longfin Inshore Squid

SPECIES • *Loligo pealeii*

These squid live in schools and are caught commercially in some areas. They are attracted to artificial light, which fishermen may use to draw them to the surface at night.

VITAL STATISTICS

WEIGHT	5–6.7 oz (140–190 g); males larger
LENGTH	Main part of the body measures 15.7–19.6 in (40–50 cm)
SEXUAL MATURITY	14–20 months
INCUBATION PERIOD	About 27 days, with the *larvae* (immature forms) drifting with the current
NUMBER OF EGGS	200, laid in packets on the seabed in inshore waters
DIET	Preys on shrimp, other squid, and fish
LIFE SPAN	2–3 years

WHERE IN THE WORLD?

Found in the North Atlantic, ranging from the coast of Newfoundland south through the Caribbean to Venezuela in South America.

ANIMAL FACTS

Longfin inshore squid are known for being fast and maneuverable swimmers. They move through the water using jet propulsion, by forcing water through a tube called a siphon. Their swimming ability is their main protection from *predators* (hunting animals). However, they also can release clouds of ink to blind predators. Like all squid, longfin inshore squid have three hearts. People catch these squids for food. They also are important for medical research. The squids have unusually large nerve cells, which makes such cells easier to study.

COLORATION
Like other squid, this *species* (kind) can quickly change color if threatened or to signal other squids.

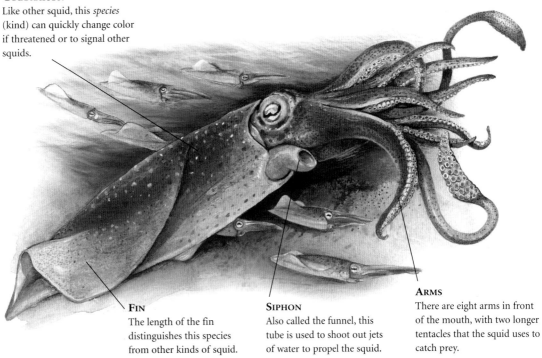

FIN
The length of the fin distinguishes this species from other kinds of squid.

SIPHON
Also called the funnel, this tube is used to shoot out jets of water to propel the squid.

ARMS
There are eight arms in front of the mouth, with two longer tentacles that the squid uses to catch prey.

MATING
Males court females by flashing complex patterns across their bodies, after which they mate and the female lays eggs.

ESCAPE FROM DANGER
Sharks prey on these squid, but the squids can maneuver so quickly that they are often able to escape their pursuers.

HOW BIG IS IT?

Common Cuttlefish

VITAL STATISTICS

WEIGHT	Up to 11 lb (4.9 kg)
LENGTH	Mantle 20-30 in (50-76.2 cm)
SEXUAL MATURITY	1–2 years
NUMBER OF EGGS	20–35, fertilized internally; both sexes die after spawning
HATCHING PERIOD	About 2 months, depending on the sea temperature
DIET	Crabs, shrimp, fish, and other prey
LIFE SPAN	1–2 years

ANIMAL FACTS

Cuttlefish usually rest on the sea floor, waiting to ambush prey. When threatened by a *predator* (hunting animal), they use jet propulsion to escape. They can also squirt a cloud of ink, to blind and confuse pursuers. This ink, which is called sepia, was once an important source of writing ink. Cuttlefish can change the color of their skin in an instant to blend in with their surroundings or to communicate with other cuttlefish. For example, a male attracts females by rapidly passing bands of color down his body. Cuttlefish are closely related to octopuses and squids. There are more than 100 *species* (kinds).

A cuttlefish makes a getaway from an eel by spraying ink, which is called sepia.

Cuttlefish are intelligent animals that can change their skin color and patterning in less than a second. This behavior enables them to blend in with their surroundings and to signal other cuttlefish.

WHERE IN THE WORLD?

Can be found throughout the Baltic and North seas, south to Spain and the Mediterranean, and along the west coast of Africa to the southern tip of the continent.

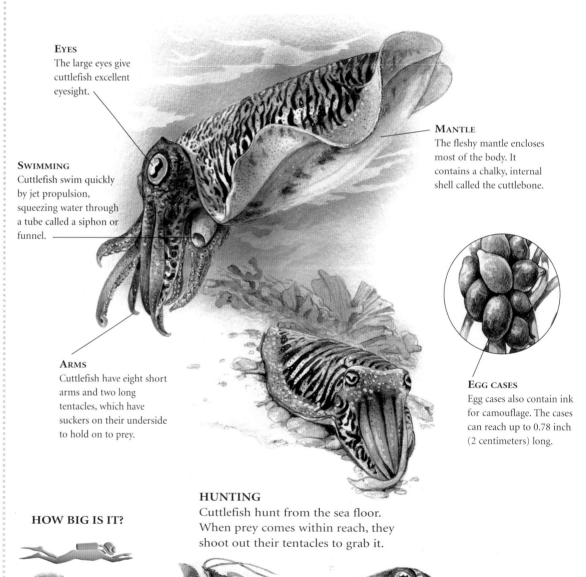

EYES
The large eyes give cuttlefish excellent eyesight.

SWIMMING
Cuttlefish swim quickly by jet propulsion, squeezing water through a tube called a siphon or funnel.

MANTLE
The fleshy mantle encloses most of the body. It contains a chalky, internal shell called the cuttlebone.

ARMS
Cuttlefish have eight short arms and two long tentacles, which have suckers on their underside to hold on to prey.

EGG CASES
Egg cases also contain ink for camouflage. The cases can reach up to 0.78 inch (2 centimeters) long.

HOW BIG IS IT?

HUNTING
Cuttlefish hunt from the sea floor. When prey comes within reach, they shoot out their tentacles to grab it.

Giant Clam

VITAL STATISTICS

HABITAT	Tropical reefs, down to 50 ft (15 m)
LENGTH	Up to 4 ft (1.2 m)
SEXUAL MATURITY	About 7 years
HATCHING	Within 24–48 hours; drift with the currents for about a week; young retain a foot for movement until they are 1 in (2.5 cm) long
EGGS	500 million may be released by a clam at a single spawning
DIET	Symbiotic relationship with algae; also eats *plankton* (tiny organisms)
LIFE SPAN	Over 100 years

The giant clam is the largest of all shellfish. It has a *symbiotic* (dependent) relationship with algae, providing them with a home in exchange for food. The clam also filters the water to feed on tiny animals.

WHERE IN THE WORLD?

Limited to warmer waters, extending through the Indian Ocean and east to southern parts of the Pacific to as far north as the Philippines.

ANIMAL FACTS

The algae the giant clam houses in its body limit where it can grow. Young clams must settle on a relatively shallow area of the ocean floor, where there is plentiful sunlight. The algae use the energy in sunlight to create their own food. They provide some of this food for the giant clam. In this way, the symbiotic relationship benefits both the giant clam and algae. The numbers of giant clams have fallen because people have harvested them for their shells.

The inside of the giant clam looks different when the shell is partially closed.

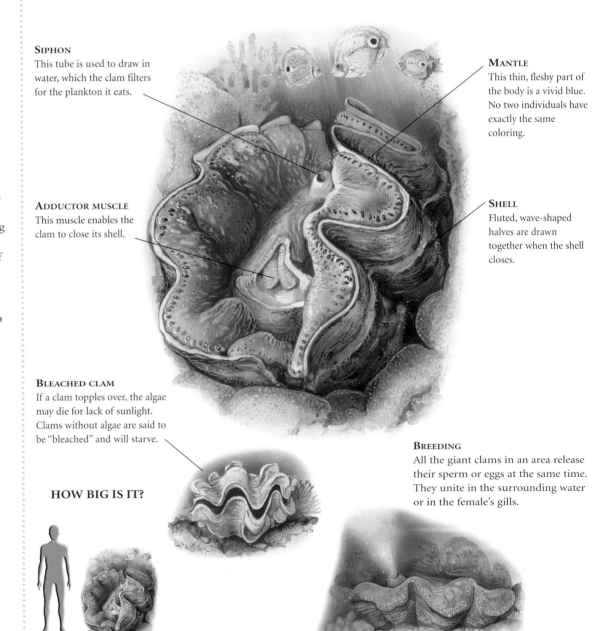

SIPHON
This tube is used to draw in water, which the clam filters for the plankton it eats.

MANTLE
This thin, fleshy part of the body is a vivid blue. No two individuals have exactly the same coloring.

ADDUCTOR MUSCLE
This muscle enables the clam to close its shell.

SHELL
Fluted, wave-shaped halves are drawn together when the shell closes.

BLEACHED CLAM
If a clam topples over, the algae may die for lack of sunlight. Clams without algae are said to be "bleached" and will starve.

BREEDING
All the giant clams in an area release their sperm or eggs at the same time. They unite in the surrounding water or in the female's gills.

HOW BIG IS IT?

Common Whelk

SPECIES • *Buccinum undatum*

These ocean snails are *predators* (hunting animals) that rely on their remarkable sense of smell to find food. They draw water in through a tube and then pass it over an organ that detects scents.

VITAL STATISTICS

LENGTH	About 4 in (10 cm) tall and 2.3 in (6 cm) wide
SEXUAL MATURITY	1–2 years
EGGS	Laid in capsules, each containing about 1,000 eggs
DEVELOPMENTAL PERIOD	Lasts several months, with miniature whelks emerging from the egg capsules
HABITAT	Usually shallow coastal waters
DIET	Crabs, bivalves, and other *invertebrates* (animals without backbones); also scavenges dead and decaying animals
LIFE SPAN	Up to 10 years

ANIMAL FACTS

Whelks have a long, tonguelike organ called the radula. The radula is covered in rows of small teeth and can be used to drill into the shell of a crab or bivalve. The whelk then sucks up the soft flesh within. Female whelks package their eggs in capsules for protection. A capsule typically contain about 1,000 eggs. But only 10 of these eggs will develop into whelks. The rest serve as food for the others. Fishermen have traditionally used egg capsules as "sea soap" to wash their hands. Discarded whelk shells are often taken up and used for shelter by hermit crabs.

WHERE IN THE WORLD?

Found along coastlines in the North Atlantic, from New Jersey north to Greenland and east to the British Isles and France.

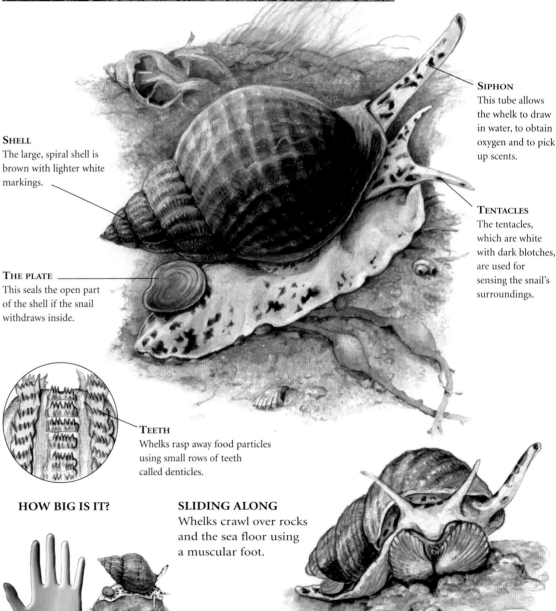

SIPHON
This tube allows the whelk to draw in water, to obtain oxygen and to pick up scents.

TENTACLES
The tentacles, which are white with dark blotches, are used for sensing the snail's surroundings.

SHELL
The large, spiral shell is brown with lighter white markings.

THE PLATE
This seals the open part of the shell if the snail withdraws inside.

TEETH
Whelks rasp away food particles using small rows of teeth called denticles.

HOW BIG IS IT?

SLIDING ALONG
Whelks crawl over rocks and the sea floor using a muscular foot.

Triton

These large snails are named after the son of the Greek sea god Poseidon, who is often portrayed holding the triton's distinctive, attractive shell. Tritons are aggressive *predators* (hunters) of starfish.

VITAL STATISTICS

LENGTH	Up to 19 in (50 cm) tall and 7 in (18 cm) wide
SEXUAL MATURITY	1–2 years
EGGS	Laid in capsules; may be guarded until they hatch in about 2 months
DEVELOPMENTAL PERIOD	Young drift with the plankton for about 3 months
HABITAT	Usually found in relatively shallow and coastal waters
DIET	*Invertebrates* (animals without backbones), especially starfish
LIFE SPAN	Over 10 years

ANIMAL FACTS

Tritons are a starfish's worst nightmare. Their pursuit of the starfish may look slow to our eyes, but the starfish has little hope of escaping the faster triton. The snail latches on to its prey, using its rough mouthparts to break open the starfish's skin. It then injects a paralyzing saliva and eats the soft body parts. Tritons are especially welcome on Australia's Great Barrier Reef, where they are one of the few predators that attack the crown-of-thorns starfish. These large starfish, which are covered in *venomous* (poisonous) spines, feed on corals. They have caused much damage to the reef.

WHERE IN THE WORLD?

Widely distributed in the world's oceans, in temperate and tropical seas. The largest species lives in the Indo-Pacific region.

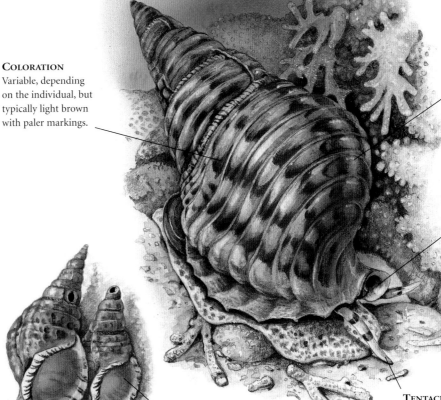

COLORATION
Variable, depending on the individual, but typically light brown with paler markings.

SHELL
The shell is covered by conspicuous ridges and extends into a cone-shaped structure known as the spire.

SHELL FOLD
This provides the tube through which the snail draws in water, for its gills.

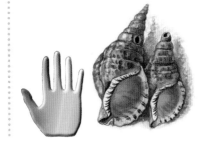

MUSICAL INSTRUMENTS
People have traditionally converted large triton shells into musical instruments by drilling holes in them.

TENTACLES
The eyes are at the base of these feelers, which extend from under the shell.

HOW BIG IS IT?

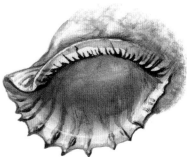

INNER SHELL
The outer lip is thickened, with a distinctive fold. The inner part of the shell is orange in color.

Red-Knobbed Starfish

VITAL STATISTICS

HABITAT	Tropical reefs, to depths of about 100 ft (30 m)
LENGTH	Maximum span from the tip of one arm to another is 12 in (30 cm)
SEXUAL MATURITY	1 year
HATCHING	After hatching, drifts with the currents for several months
EGGS	External fertilization; millions of eggs may be released by a single female
DIET	Mainly mussels and clams, pulled apart with the arms
LIFE SPAN	3–5 years

Starfish are close relatives of sea urchins and sand dollars. Most starfish have five arms, though some *species* (kinds) have more. One species that lives near Antarctica can have more than 50 arms.

WHERE IN THE WORLD?

Range extends from the Red Sea, across the Indian Ocean and around Indonesia, eastward into the Pacific tropics.

ANIMAL FACTS

If a starfish loses one of its arms, it may grow another over time. It is even possible for two starfish to regrow from a single individual that was cut in half. Starfish have an eye at the end of each arm, though these eyes can sense only light or dark. The arms are strengthened by a type of skeleton made up of bony plates located just beneath the skin. Scientists have identified nearly 2,000 species of starfish. Some species are harmful to coral reefs.

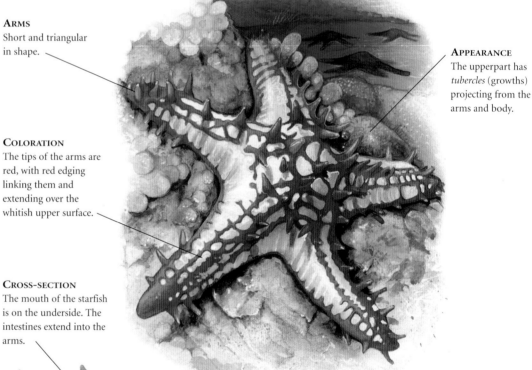

ARMS
Short and triangular in shape.

APPEARANCE
The upperpart has *tubercles* (growths) projecting from the arms and body.

COLORATION
The tips of the arms are red, with red edging linking them and extending over the whitish upper surface.

CROSS-SECTION
The mouth of the starfish is on the underside. The intestines extend into the arms.

TUBE FEET
The tube feet on the underside of a starfish help the animal grip prey and move around.

HOW BIG IS IT?

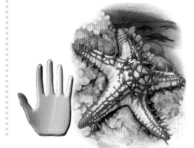

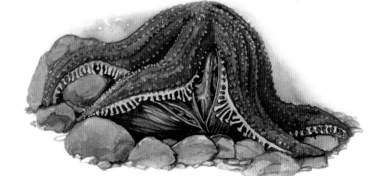

Sea Urchin

VITAL STATISTICS

LENGTH	2-10 in (5-25 cm)
SEXUAL MATURITY	2–5 years
NUMBER OF EGGS	Several million, released at once
INCUBATION PERIOD	Eggs develop into tiny *larvae* (immature forms), which drift with the currents
HABITAT	The seabed, often in shallow water
DIET	Feeds largely on algae but may also prey on sponges and mussels
LIFE SPAN	Up to 200 years

ANIMAL FACTS

There are hundreds of *species* (kinds) of urchins. Their name is an Old English word for *hedgehogs*, which they resemble. Stepping on a sea urchin can be painful. The spines often break off in the flesh and may contain *venom* (poison). If some of the spines are touched gently, the neighboring spines lean toward the point of contact. Sea urchins move by pushing with their spines or using tiny tube feet on the underside of the body.

The body parts of sea urchins and such close relatives as sand dollars are arranged around the center of the animal, like the spokes of a wheel.

Sea urchins have a covering of spines that protects them from *predators* (hunting animals). This physical *adaptation* (characteristic) has enabled sea urchins to thrive for at least 450 million years.

WHERE IN THE WORLD?

Members of this group live in oceans throughout the world but are most common in tropical seas, found on or near coral reefs.

SPINES
These protect the sea urchin's body. Their length varies between different groups. Some sea urchins also use their tube feet to cover themselves with broken shell bits and seaweed in an attempt to hide from predators.

BODY
The body is protected by the encircling spines, so distinctive features are not clearly visible.

MOUTH AND GILLS
The vulnerable mouth and gills are on the underside of the animal, where they are protected from predators. The animal scrapes up food using a set of five hard teeth.

COLORATION
Common colors include shades of green, brown, purple, and red. Many are black.

CROSS-SECTION
The typical internal structure of a sea urchin is seen here. The purplish area is the animal's intestines.

HOW BIG IS IT?

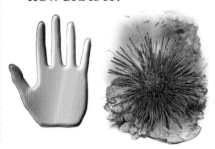

DANGEROUS LIVING
Some fish have evolved a strategy for eating sea urchins—they attack the vulnerable underside of the body. To avoid the spines, they blow the urchin off the seabed with a jet of water and then seize it from below.

North Atlantic Right Whale

SPECIES • *Eubalaena glacialis*

VITAL STATISTICS

WEIGHT	Up to 70 tons (63.5 metric tons); females are heavier
LENGTH	46–56 ft (14–17 m)
SEXUAL MATURITY	6–10 years
LENGTH OF PREGNANCY	About 365 days; females give birth once every 3–5 years
NUMBER OF OFFSPRING	1; weaning occurs at 8–12 months
DIET	Filters the water for *plankton* (tiny organisms)
LIFE SPAN	Likely to be 50–100 years

Right whales got their name because whalers regarded them as the "right" whale to hunt. Nearly hunted to extinction, these whales have been protected since the 1930's. Nevertheless, their numbers remain small.

WHERE IN THE WORLD?

Ranges through the North Atlantic Ocean along the eastern coast of North America. Was once common in European waters from the Iberian Peninsula to Scandinavia.

ANIMAL FACTS

Although North Atlantic right whales are protected from whaling, many are still killed accidentally by human beings. The leading causes of death are drowning after becoming entangled in fishing nets and strikes by ships. To reduce ship strikes, the United States has set seasonal speed limits on ships, so the whales have time to move out of the way. Right whales make seasonal migrations, spending the winter off the coast of North Carolina with newborn calves. They travel to polar waters to feed during the summer.

Males nuzzle females with their snouts during the breeding season.

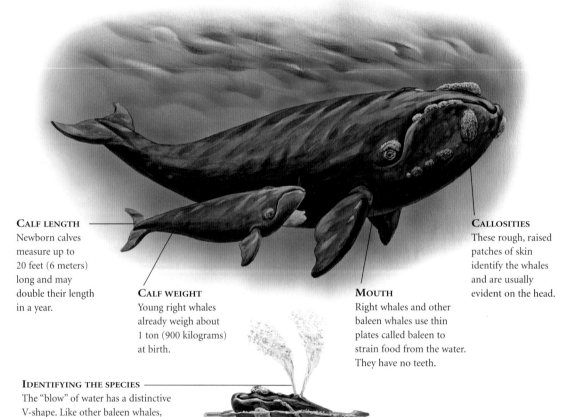

CALF LENGTH
Newborn calves measure up to 20 feet (6 meters) long and may double their length in a year.

CALF WEIGHT
Young right whales already weigh about 1 ton (900 kilograms) at birth.

MOUTH
Right whales and other baleen whales use thin plates called baleen to strain food from the water. They have no teeth.

CALLOSITIES
These rough, raised patches of skin identify the whales and are usually evident on the head.

IDENTIFYING THE SPECIES
The "blow" of water has a distinctive V-shape. Like other baleen whales, right whales have two blowholes.

HOW BIG IS IT?

BREACHING
Whales are acrobats who often *breach* (leap from the water and spin then dive back in). Scientists do not know why whales breach, but it may be a form of communication.

Blue Whale

VITAL STATISTICS

WEIGHT	Up to 147 tons (133.3 metric tons); females are much heavier
LENGTH	82–100 ft (25–30 m)
SEXUAL MATURITY	6–10 years
LENGTH OF PREGNANCY	About 365 days; females give birth once every 3–5 years
NUMBER OF OFFSPRING	1; weaning occurs at 8–12 months
DIET	Filters the water for tiny, shrimplike krill
LIFE SPAN	Up to 110 years

ANIMAL FACTS

These giant animals have appetites to match. An individual blue whale may eat up to 4 tons (3.6 metric tons) of krill each day. That's about 40 million krill! Blue whales live in small groups of two or three individuals. They swim at about 12 miles (19 kilometers) per hour, though they can travel up to 30 miles (48 kilometers) per hour. Whaling nearly led to the extinction of these giants. Although they have been protected by international law since 1966, they remain endangered. Scientists believe there are 10,000 to 25,000 blue whales alive today. They once numbered in the hundreds of thousands.

Blue whales are the largest animals that have ever lived on Earth, weighing far more than even the largest dinosaurs. These giants feed on some of the smallest animals—tiny, shrimplike krill.

WHERE IN THE WORLD?

Ranges widely through the world's oceans, but has distinct populations in the North Atlantic, in the North Pacific, and near Antarctica.

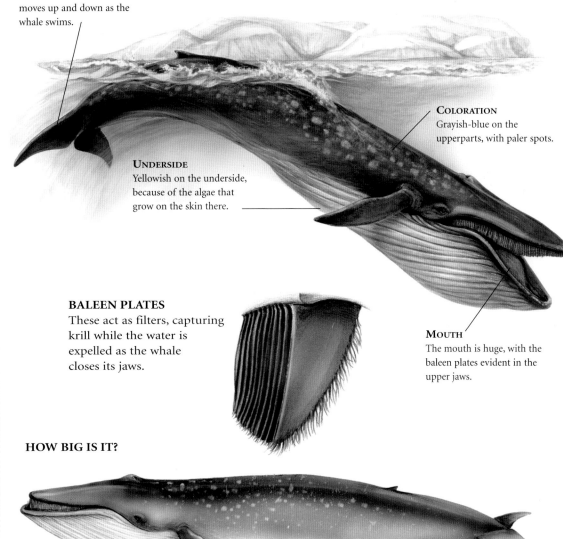

TAIL
Flat, broad, and thick, the tail moves up and down as the whale swims.

UNDERSIDE
Yellowish on the underside, because of the algae that grow on the skin there.

COLORATION
Grayish-blue on the upperparts, with paler spots.

BALEEN PLATES
These act as filters, capturing krill while the water is expelled as the whale closes its jaws.

MOUTH
The mouth is huge, with the baleen plates evident in the upper jaws.

HOW BIG IS IT?

Humpback Whale

VITAL STATISTICS

WEIGHT	22–36 tons (19.9–32.6 metric tons); females are much heavier
LENGTH	40–50 ft (12–15 m)
SEXUAL MATURITY	6–10 years
LENGTH OF PREGNANCY	About 365 days; females give birth once every 2–3 years
NUMBER OF OFFSPRING	1; weaning occurs at about 12 months
DIET	Filters the water for shrimplike krill; also eats small fish
LIFE SPAN	Up to 100 years

ANIMAL FACTS

The remarkable song of the male humpback whale is uttered repeatedly for hours, with each segment lasting up to 20 minutes. The singing probably helps the whales to keep in touch with one another when separated in the oceans. Their song patterns are distinctive and change over time. Humpbacks are often seen jumping above the water, a behavior called breaching. Like singing, breaching may be part of their courtship ritual. Females typically migrate to warmer areas in the winter, to give birth to their calves. In the summer, they return to cooler waters to feed. These whales were nearly hunted to extinction, but their numbers have recovered since they were protected in 1966.

These baleen whales are relatively easy to spot because they often come quite close to shore, swim at the surface, and jump above the waves.

WHERE IN THE WORLD?

Ranges worldwide, migrating between tropical waters in the winter and polar waters in the summer.

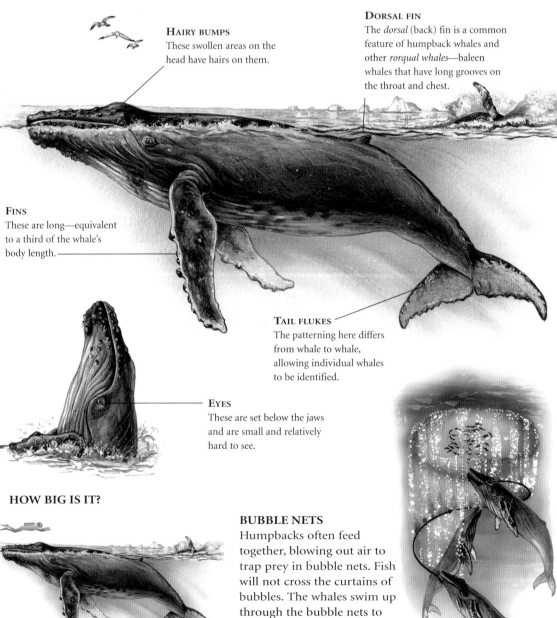

HAIRY BUMPS
These swollen areas on the head have hairs on them.

DORSAL FIN
The *dorsal* (back) fin is a common feature of humpback whales and other *rorqual whales*—baleen whales that have long grooves on the throat and chest.

FINS
These are long—equivalent to a third of the whale's body length.

TAIL FLUKES
The patterning here differs from whale to whale, allowing individual whales to be identified.

EYES
These are set below the jaws and are small and relatively hard to see.

HOW BIG IS IT?

BUBBLE NETS
Humpbacks often feed together, blowing out air to trap prey in bubble nets. Fish will not cross the curtains of bubbles. The whales swim up through the bubble nets to gobble up many fish at once.

Sperm Whale

SPECIES • *Physeter catodon*

Sperm whales are the largest of the toothed whales. The classic novel *Moby-Dick* (1851) is the story of a whaling captain's obsessive hunt for a fierce white sperm whale.

VITAL STATISTICS

WEIGHT	14–40 tons (12.7–36 metric tons); males are at least a third bigger
LENGTH	40–60 ft (12–18 m); individuals up to 68 ft (20.5 m) existed until recently
SEXUAL MATURITY	Females 8–11 years; males around 10 years
LENGTH OF PREGNANCY	About 18 months
NUMBER OF OFFSPRING	1; weaning takes about 2 years
DIET	Giant squid and octopus
LIFE SPAN	Can be 75 years

WHERE IN THE WORLD?

Ranges throughout the world's oceans, occurring in areas of deep water. Males tend to migrate toward the poles in summer.

ANIMAL FACTS

These whales are able to dive to tremendous depths, reaching 9,840 feet (3,000 meters) below the surface. They can stay submerged for up to two hours. It is thought that this allows them to prey on giant squid, which live in the cold depths. In fact, people had noted scars caused by suckers on the sides of sperm whales before anyone had ever seen giant squids. These scars provide evidence of the epic battles that occur between these animals in the deep.

A sperm whale battles with a giant squid, which can reach 53 feet (16 meters) in length.

BACK
Instead of a *dorsal* (back) fin, the whale has a series of wavy humps that run down the middle of the back.

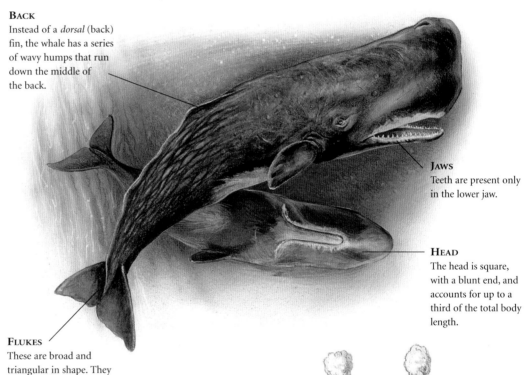

JAWS
Teeth are present only in the lower jaw.

HEAD
The head is square, with a blunt end, and accounts for up to a third of the total body length.

FLUKES
These are broad and triangular in shape. They are lifted out of the water just before a dive.

HOW BIG IS IT?

BLOWHOLE
Like other toothed whales, the sperm whale has one blowhole. But the blowhole is closer to the front of the head than in other toothed whales. The blow itself is directed forward, enabling these whales to be recognized from a distance.

Harbor Porpoise

VITAL STATISTICS

WEIGHT	130–200 lb (60–90 kg); females are slightly larger
LENGTH	5–6 ft (1.5–1.8 m)
SEXUAL MATURITY	3–4 years
LENGTH OF PREGNANCY	Around 341 days; calves are about 27 in (71 cm) long at birth
NUMBER OF OFFSPRING	1; weaning takes about 8 months
DIET	Hunts such smaller fish as whiting, herring, pollock, and sardines, as well as squid
LIFE SPAN	10–20 years

ANIMAL FACTS

Living close to the shore can be hazardous for these porpoises, as they may die if they become tangled in fishing nets. Such accidents have led to a major decline in their populations in the Baltic and Black seas. They are usually seen in small groups that include up to 10 individuals. Members of the group work together to find food. A porpoise must eat up to 10 percent of its body weight daily. Harbor porpoises make an unusual snuffling sound when surfacing.

Harbor porpoises are hunted by killer whales.

Small in size and relatively shy by nature, these porpoises live in coastal waters, often frequenting bays and sometimes swimming up the mouths of rivers.

WHERE IN THE WORLD?

Lives in northern coastal waters in both the Atlantic and Pacific oceans. Also present in the Black and Baltic seas.

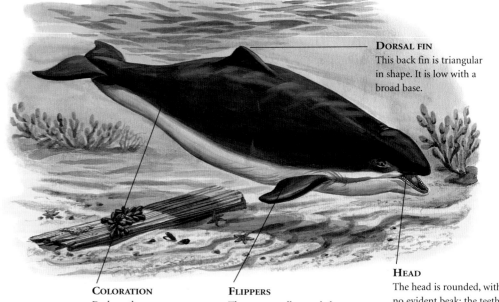

DORSAL FIN
This back fin is triangular in shape. It is low with a broad base.

COLORATION
Dark on the upperparts, with a whitish underside.

FLIPPERS
These are small, rounded, and dark in color, with a dark stripe extending forward toward the eyes.

HEAD
The head is rounded, with no evident beak; the teeth are small in the jaws.

TAIL FIRST
The young porpoise is born tail-first and then helped up to the surface by its mother so that it can breathe air.

HOW BIG IS IT?

Long-Finned Pilot Whale

SPECIES • *Globicephala melas*

VITAL STATISTICS

WEIGHT	1.3–2.6 tons (1.2–2.4 metric tons); males are much bigger
LENGTH	16–20 ft (4.88–6.10 m)
SEXUAL MATURITY	Females 6–7 years; males around 12 years
LENGTH OF PREGNANCY	About 310 days
NUMBER OF OFFSPRING	1; weaning typically occurs by 2 years old
DIET	Feeds mainly on squid, as well as octopus, cuttlefish, and herring
LIFE SPAN	Over 50 years

ANIMAL FACTS

There are two *species* (kinds) of pilot whales, which can be distinguished by the length of their fins. Pods of pilot whales can include up to 100 individuals. The pods are led by older females. The pods work together to raise young, with some members watching the young so mothers can dive to feed. Males in the group are likely to join for a period and then move on. The males fight among themselves to mate with females. They can ram each other and bite, sometimes leaving permanent scars.

Rounded head of the pilot whale (left) compared with the pointed head of a true whale (right)

Despite their name, pilot whales are actually dolphins. Highly social by nature, they live in tight-knit groups called pods. Members of the pod communicate using high-pitched whistles.

WHERE IN THE WORLD?

Found in cool waters, from South America, South Africa, and Australia to the Antarctic. Also found in the North Atlantic and parts of the Mediterranean.

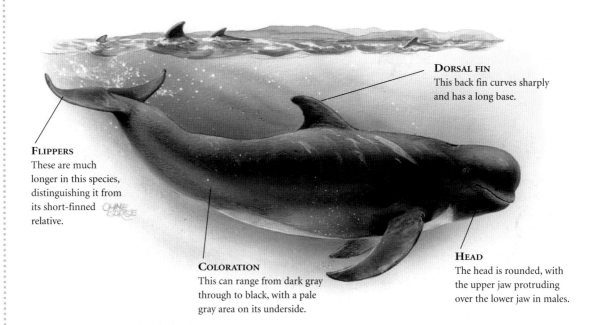

DORSAL FIN
This back fin curves sharply and has a long base.

FLIPPERS
These are much longer in this species, distinguishing it from its short-finned relative.

COLORATION
This can range from dark gray through to black, with a pale gray area on its underside.

HEAD
The head is rounded, with the upper jaw protruding over the lower jaw in males.

SOFT FOOD
Ink-spurting squid are among the animals hunted by pilot whales. The whales have only about 40 teeth in their jaws, compared with more than 100 teeth in fish-eating dolphins.

MASS STRANDINGS
Pilot whales sometimes beach themselves, possibly because of illness or confusion caused by *sonar* (sound) signals from ocean vessels.

HOW BIG IS IT?

Killer Whale

VITAL STATISTICS

WEIGHT	4–9 tons (3.6–8.2 metric tons); males are much bigger
LENGTH	19–27 ft (6–8 m)
SEXUAL MATURITY	10–18 years; females tend to mature earlier
LENGTH OF PREGNANCY	400–520 days
NUMBER OF OFFSPRING	1; weaning occurs after 13–17 months
DIET	Feeds mainly on larger *vertebrates* (animals with backbones), including sea lions, penguins, and whales; also hunts squid
LIFE SPAN	Can be over 80 years

Killer whales, also known as orcas, are top *predators* (hunting animals) in the oceans. They feed on a variety of large animals, including whales. Killer whales are actually the largest kind of dolphin.

WHERE IN THE WORLD?

Lives widely throughout the world's oceans, often close to the shore, but is most common in temperate and polar regions.

ANIMAL FACTS

Killer whales live in groups known as pods. Pods often work together to hunt. Pods roam through the oceans, traveling up to 100 miles (160 kilometers) per day. However, some killer whales stay in one place, especially in areas where fish are plentiful. The pod is led by an older female. Pod members keep in touch with each other through high-pitched sounds. They also use these sounds like sonar, to help them find prey. This ability is called echolocation.

DORSAL FIN
This back fin can be up to 6 feet (1.8 meters) tall. It is triangular in males and shorter and curved in females and the young of both sexes.

PATTERNING
All killer whales are black on top and have white undersides. But individuals look different enough to be recognized easily.

FLIPPERS
The flippers are broad, reaching up to 3 feet (0.91 meter) wide and 6 feet (1.8 meters) long. They have rounded tips.

The mouth is straight, rather than curved.

HOW BIG IS IT?

GROUP HUNTING
Killer whales are called "wolves of the sea" because of the way they hunt as a pack, surrounding their prey.

Commerson's Dolphin

Commerson's dolphins are among the smallest of all dolphins. Because of the black and white shading of the adults, these dolphins are sometimes called "skunk dolphins" or "panda dolphins."

VITAL STATISTICS

WEIGHT	77–132 lb (35–60 kg)
LENGTH	4–5.6 ft (1.2–1.7 m)
SEXUAL MATURITY	6–9 years
LENGTH OF PREGNANCY	About 334 days; young are large— nearly half the size of their mothers at birth
NUMBER OF OFFSPRING	1; weaning may take over a year
DIET	Feeds on a variety of fish and squid, and also shrimp
LIFE SPAN	Up to 18 years; more than 26 years in captivity

ANIMAL FACTS

These mammals live relatively close to the shore and sometimes enter coastal inlets. People often spot them leaping from the water. The dolphins also accompany boats. They may swim upside down at the surface, perhaps as a way of spotting prey. Females nurse their young through slits on the belly, for as long as a year. This *species* (kind) is named after the French naturalist Philibert Commerçon, who first documented them in the Straits of Magellan off South America in 1766.

WHERE IN THE WORLD?

Two distinct populations exist. The largest is off southern South America and the Falkland Islands. Another population lives around the Kerguelen Islands in the southern Indian Ocean.

DORSAL FIN
This is long and straight along its upper surface and ends in a curved tip.

FACE
The dolphins have a streamlined, rounded face with broad jaws.

PATTERNING
The throat and body are black. The snout, fins, and tail are black.

FLUKE
The tail fin in these dolphins has a notch in the middle of its outer edge.

MALES AND FEMALES
Both males and females have black markings on their undersides. In males, the marking looks like a teardrop. In females, it is shaped like an arrowhead.

HOW BIG IS IT?

COLOR SHIFTS
Young are born gray, black, and brown, and then become black and gray. The gray areas eventually become white.

Short-Beaked Common Dolphin

SPECIES • *Delphinus delphis*

These dolphins have been admired since ancient times for the assistance they sometimes give to people lost at sea, helping guide them to shore and even protecting them from sharks.

VITAL STATISTICS

WEIGHT	155–242 lb (70–110 kg)
LENGTH	About 6–8 ft (1.8–2.4 m)
SEXUAL MATURITY	4–5 years; males mature slightly earlier than females
LENGTH OF PREGNANCY	About 310 days
NUMBER OF OFFSPRING	1; weaning may take about a year
DIET	Feeds on a variety of small schooling fish, including sardines and squid
LIFE SPAN	Up to 20 years; more than 34 in captivity

WHERE IN THE WORLD?

Lives in many warm and tropical areas around the world, usually relatively near the coasts. Also found in the Mediterranean and Black seas.

ANIMAL FACTS

These mammals live in groups called schools. The schools range in size from a few dolphins up to 100,000, depending on the time of year and availability of food. The dolphins care for sick members of the school, helping them to surface so they can breathe. Within the school, adults teach the young how to hunt. The school works together to hunt prey, sometimes driving fish toward an ambush. They also blow out air to create "bubble nets" that trap fish in a tight ball, making it easy for the swift dolphins to swoop in on their prey.

FACIAL FEATURES
The beak is sharply divided from the lower forehead by a deep groove. The mouth contains 40 or more teeth.

DORSAL FIN
This is tall and held erect, curving back on its upper surface to a point.

FLANKS
A pale yellow or buff area is visible toward the front, with gray toward the rear and white below.

COLORATION
Four colors are apparent over the body, with black prominent along the back.

HOW BIG IS IT?

ECHOLOCATION
Like other dolphins, these animals use the echoes from the rapid clicking sounds they make to sense their surroundings. Some scientists believe the dolphins can even stun fish with the powerful sounds they make.

GIVING BIRTH
The female gives birth tail-first, preventing her calf from trying to breathe prematurely. After the birth, the mother helps her calf to the surface to breathe air.

Hooded Seal

The pouch on the head of a mature male hooded seal explains the animal's name. The pouch can expand to about twice the size of a football to attract females and warn off other males.

VITAL STATISTICS

WEIGHT	771–992 lb (350–450 kg); males are heavier
LENGTH	6.5–9.8 ft (2–3 m)
SEXUAL MATURITY	Females 3–6 years; males 5–7 years
LENGTH OF PREGNANCY	341–365 days
NUMBER OF OFFSPRING	1; weaning occurs in 5 to 12 days—the shortest period of any mammal
DIET	Hunts fish including herring and cod, as well as squid, starfish, and shellfish, depending on availability
LIFE SPAN	30–35 years

ANIMAL FACTS

The growth of young hooded seal pups is amazing. They nurse for only 5 to 12 days but double their weight in that time. This growth is possible because the mother's milk is rich, with about 65 percent fat. The pup's coat is bluish-gray at first. It is shed and replaced at 14 months. The number of hooded seals has greatly declined, largely because of decades of hunting for the pelts of the pups.

Hooded seals dive to depths of 3,280 feet (1,000 meters) and can stay submerged for more than 50 minutes.

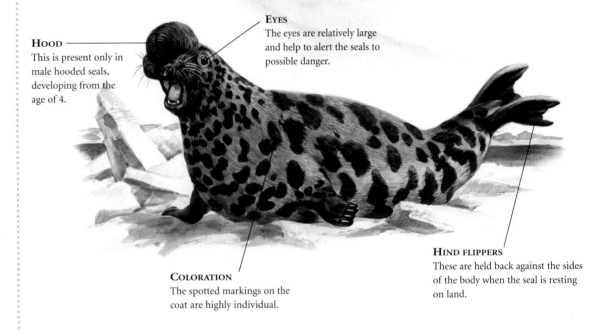

WHERE IN THE WORLD?

Found in the North Atlantic, from Canada to Norway. Sometimes travels to Alaska, Guadeloupe, or the Canary Islands.

HOOD
This is present only in male hooded seals, developing from the age of 4.

EYES
The eyes are relatively large and help to alert the seals to possible danger.

COLORATION
The spotted markings on the coat are highly individual.

HIND FLIPPERS
These are held back against the sides of the body when the seal is resting on land.

INTIMIDATION BY BALLOON
Male hooded seals also can inflate their nasal cavity, pushing it out through their nostrils, to threaten other males or to attract females.

HOW BIG IS IT?

Mediterranean Monk Seal

SPECIES · *Monachus monachus*

The Mediterranean monk seal is the most endangered seal in the world, with fewer than 500 surviving. Scientists are working to save this species before it disappears forever.

VITAL STATISTICS

WEIGHT	551–661 lb (250–300 kg)
LENGTH	7.8–9.1 ft (2.4–2.8 m)
SEXUAL MATURITY	Females 4–6 years; males 5–6 years
LENGTH OF PREGNANCY	About 341 days; mating takes place in the water
NUMBER OF OFFSPRING	1; weaning occurs by 17 weeks
DIET	Feeds on a variety of fish, such as sardines, tuna and mullet; also eats lobsters, octopus, and squid
LIFE SPAN	20–30 years

ANIMAL FACTS

Mediterranean monk seals were once plentiful throughout the region, but they now live in only a small part of this range. The seals face a number of major threats. Fishermen sometimes kill the seals because they think the seals compete for fish. The seals also become entangled in fishing nets. Habitat destruction is another threat. Pollution in the form of oil spills and sewage also threatens their survival. Huge numbers of the seals died in 1996, due either to disease or to *toxins* (poisons) released by *plankton* (tiny organisms). The seals are now protected by law.

The skull of a Mediterranean monk seal

WHERE IN THE WORLD?

Lives in the eastern Mediterranean Sea, around Greece and Turkey. Small numbers survive on the northwestern coast of Africa.

FLIPPERS
The flippers are short and end in short claws.

EARS
There are no external earflaps on the ears.

COAT LENGTH
The fur of the Mediterranean monk seal is shorter than that of any other seal.

COLORATION
Females are brownish with lighter underparts and blotching, while males are black, with white on the belly.

NOSTRILS
These are prominent, long, and pointed upwards.

These seals live relatively close to shore.

HOW BIG IS IT?

BIRTHING CAVES
Females tend to give birth along inaccessible parts of coastline, often seeking out the relative safety of caves.

Common Seal

VITAL STATISTICS

WEIGHT	99–375 lb (45–170 kg); males are heavier
LENGTH	4–6.3 ft (1.2–1.9 m)
SEXUAL MATURITY	Females 4–6 years; males 5–6 years
LENGTH OF PREGNANCY	About 225 days; development only starts about 4.5 months after fertilization
NUMBER OF OFFSPRING	1; weaning occurs at around 28 days
DIET	Feeds mainly on fish, including sand eels and herring, also mollusks, shrimp, and squid
LIFE SPAN	20–30 years; males typically have a shorter life span

ANIMAL FACTS

Common seals are known for their curiosity. They may approach beaches or boats for a closer look at people. The young can swim and dive within hours of birth. As a result, females may give birth in relative safety on sandbanks exposed at low tide. This species has the most extensive range of any seal, and they are not considered threatened. Common seals are eaten by great white sharks and killer whales.

Common seal pup

This animal is also known as the harbor seal, because people often spot the animals in such areas. However, common seals live in a variety of coastal habitats.

WHERE IN THE WORLD?

Ranges along coastal areas throughout the Northern Hemisphere. Also present in both the North Atlantic and the North Pacific, as well as the North and Baltic seas.

COLORATION
Varies from shades of tan through brown to gray, with spots and rings evident on the top of the body.

EAR CANAL
This opening, on the side of the head behind the eye, is relatively large.

HIND FLIPPERS
As with other seals, the rear flippers provide the thrust for swimming.

FRONT FLIPPERS
Common seals are quite clumsy on land, like many other seals.

HOW BIG IS IT?

FLIPPERS
The flippers are flat and wide to aid swimming.

MOTHER AND PUP
Adopting an upright position in the water affords good all-round visibility and helps the mother to support her pup.

California Sea Lion

SPECIES • *Zalophus californianus*

These large seals are a familiar sight along the coast of California, where they gather in large *colonies* (groups) during the summer.

VITAL STATISTICS

WEIGHT	610-860 lb (275-390 kg); males are heavier
LENGTH	6–8.2 ft (1.8–2.5 m)
SEXUAL MATURITY	About 5 years, but males usually don't mate until they are older
LENGTH OF PREGNANCY	341–365 days
NUMBER OF OFFSPRING	1; weaning occurs at 26 weeks
DIET	Hunts a variety of fish, including whiting, sardines, and anchovies, as well as squid
LIFE SPAN	10–15 years in the wild; up to 30 in captivity

ANIMAL FACTS

Males have a crest on the head with a mane of longer white hair, a feature that explains why they are called sea lions. Sea lions are vocal animals, often making loud barks. California sea lions may spend days out at sea. They can dive down to depths of 900 feet (274 meters). During the breeding seasons, males guard their territories, typically for two weeks. The young grow rapidly and are already hunting with their mothers at 2 months old.

Sea lions (right) have earflaps, called pinnae, while common seals do not (left).

WHERE IN THE WORLD?

Ranges down the western coast of North America, from British Columbia south to Baja California. Also found in the Sea of Cortez.

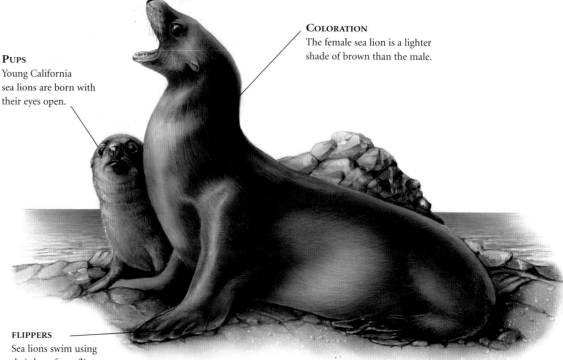

PUPS
Young California sea lions are born with their eyes open.

COLORATION
The female sea lion is a lighter shade of brown than the male.

FLIPPERS
Sea lions swim using their long front flippers, which also help them to move on land. The back flippers are used to steer.

EARS
Sea lions are considered eared seals because of the flaps covering their ears. The flaps are small and tucked close against the skull.

HOW BIG IS IT?

DIVING UNDERWATER
The flaps on the ears and nostrils of sea lions are ordinarily closed, protecting them during dives. The sea lion opens these flaps when it is on land.

Dugong

VITAL STATISTICS

WEIGHT	507–1,100 lb (230–500 kg)
LENGTH	8–10 ft (2.4–3 m)
SEXUAL MATURITY	8–18 years
LENGTH OF PREGNANCY	About 13 months; young are cream-colored at birth
NUMBER OF OFFSPRING	1; young suckle upside down beneath their mother's body; weaning occurs at around 24 months
DIET	Aquatic vegetation, browsing on underwater grasses
LIFE SPAN	Up to 70 years

ANIMAL FACTS

The grazing habits of these mammals have led to them being called sea cows, as they feed on sea grasses growing in the shallows. Dugongs live in herds or small family groups. Dugongs have short tusks of ivory, which they may use to settle disputes. Adults face few *predators* (hunting animals), but the young may be eaten by sharks, killer whales, and crocodiles. The greatest threat to dugongs comes from people. Dugongs are threatened by fishing nets, collisions with boats, and habitat destruction. Scientists fear that their numbers are falling quickly.

The dugong's snout turns downward, and the overhang allows it to dig furrows, uprooting sea grass.

Dugongs often rest near the surface, with just their heads above the water. Sailors sometimes mistook these animals for mermaids, mythical creatures said to be half human, half fish.

WHERE IN THE WORLD?

Lives throughout coastal areas in tropical seas, from East Africa and the Red Sea, across the Indian Ocean and the Pacific, south to Australia.

EYES AND EARS
The eyes are small, and dugongs have no external earflaps.

TAIL
The broad flukes move up and down to push the dugong through the water.

COLORATION
Dugongs are gray, with a sparse covering of hair over most of the body.

FLIPPERS
These measure up to 17 inches (45 centimeters) long, and are used for steering.

BREATHING
Dugongs can remain submerged for up to six minutes and need only put their nostrils above the surface to breathe.

HOW BIG IS IT?

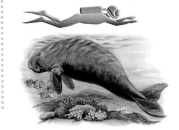

BREACHING THE SURFACE
Sometimes dugongs are observed "standing," even seeming to embrace each other.

Green Sea Turtle

VITAL STATISTICS

WEIGHT	Up to 451 lb (205 g); males weigh more
LENGTH	2.4–5 ft (0.7–1.5 m) across the middle of the shell
SEXUAL MATURITY	10–24 years
NUMBER OF EGGS	100–200, white and round
INCUBATION PERIOD	40–72 days, depending on conditions
DIET	Adults feed on algae, sea grass, and aquatic vegetation, along with jellyfish and other *invertebrates* (animals without backbones)
LIFE SPAN	Up to 80 years

These ocean reptiles spend their lives at sea, but females must return to shore to lay their eggs. Females make their nests on the same beaches where they hatched.

WHERE IN THE WORLD?

Roams throughout tropical and warm oceans, with nesting sites in the Atlantic, Pacific, and Indian oceans.

ANIMAL FACTS

The female turtle comes ashore at night to dig a nest with her hind flippers. She lays her eggs and then covers them with sand. Some weeks later, the young hatch all at once. They dig themselves out and rush to the sea, running a gauntlet of predators (hunting animals). There are so many hatchlings that predators cannot claim them all. Green sea turtles have become endangered because of human activities, including hunting, pollution, and habitat destruction.

SHELL SHAPE
The relatively flattened shell reduces water resistance, making it easier to swim.

LEGS
These are effectively paddles, but their flattened shape means the turtle has to drag itself across the sand.

UPPER SHELL
Called the carapace, this hard shell can vary from olive through brown to black in different individuals.

BREATHING
Turtles breathe air through their nostrils and must surface regularly.

TEARS
They excrete excess salt from their bodies through special tear glands.

A BRIEF LIFE
Many predators seize the hatchlings as they rush to the sea, but the turtles hatch in such large numbers that some reach safety.

Turtles (left) are adapted for swimming, while tortoises (right) walk on their toes.

HOW BIG IS IT?

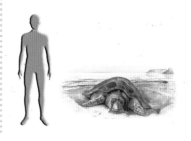

Leatherback Turtle

The leatherback is the largest living turtle. It feeds mainly on jellyfish, which have come to fill many parts of the ocean as people have killed off leatherbacks, sharks, and other jellyfish *predators* (hunters).

VITAL STATISTICS

WEIGHT	550–1,980 lb (250–900 kg)
LENGTH	4.8–5.3 ft (1.5–1.6 m) over the shell; distance between the flippers can be 8 ft 10 in (270 cm)
SEXUAL MATURITY	5–15 years
NUMBER OF EGGS	50–170, laid every 10 days up to 7 times a year; only half will hatch
INCUBATION PERIOD	55–75 days
DIET	Primarily jellyfish, but also shrimp, snails, squids, and some fish
LIFE SPAN	Perhaps 50 years

WHERE IN THE WORLD?

Lives throughout the world's oceans, up to the Arctic. Nesting beaches occur in the tropics, from French Guiana to West Africa and Papua New Guinea.

ANIMAL FACTS

Leatherbacks have become highly endangered. Many are killed when they become entangled in fishing nets. They also suffer from the pollution of the oceans—they mistake floating plastic bags for the jellyfish they eat. Swallowing plastic bags can kill leatherbacks. People also kill many of the young by harvesting the eggs. Leatherbacks range into cooler waters than other ocean turtles. This is partly a result of their large size, which helps them to maintain their core body temperature. They also have an insulating layer of fat under the skin.

Like other ocean turtles, the leatherback has no teeth, just sharp-edged jaws.

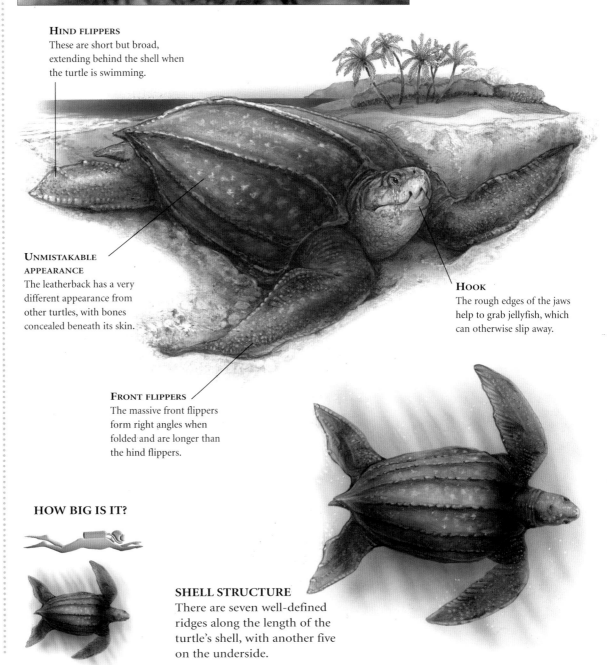

HIND FLIPPERS
These are short but broad, extending behind the shell when the turtle is swimming.

UNMISTAKABLE APPEARANCE
The leatherback has a very different appearance from other turtles, with bones concealed beneath its skin.

HOOK
The rough edges of the jaws help to grab jellyfish, which can otherwise slip away.

FRONT FLIPPERS
The massive front flippers form right angles when folded and are longer than the hind flippers.

HOW BIG IS IT?

SHELL STRUCTURE
There are seven well-defined ridges along the length of the turtle's shell, with another five on the underside.

Glossary

adaptation a characteristic of a living thing that makes it better able to survive and reproduce in its environment

algae simple organisms that live in oceans, lakes, rivers, ponds, and moist soil

anal at or near the anus

bivalve any mollusk whose shell consists of two parts hinged together so that it will open and shut like a book

breaching the action of a whale or other ocean creature in leaping free of the surface of the ocean

brood to care for eggs until they hatch

burrow a hole dug in the ground by an animal for refuge or shelter

callosity a rough, raised patch of skin on right whales

carapace a shell or bony covering on the back or part of the back of turtles, armadillos, and such crustaceans as lobsters and crabs

cartilage a bluish-white rubbery tissue found in human beings and other vertebrates

chitin a horny substance forming the hard outer covering of lobsters, crabs, and insects

crustacean an invertebrate (animal without a backbone) with jointed legs and a hard external shell

denticle a pointed projection that resembles a tooth

dorsal on or near the back

echinoderm a group of spiny-skinned sea animals with an internal bony skeleton, including starfish, brittle stars, and sea urchins

echolocation the use of sound by animals such as bats and whales to sense their surroundings; echoes from sounds the animals produce enable them to locate objects

exoskeleton any hard, external covering that protects or supports the body of an animal

fish vertebrates that live in water

gill an organ in fish and other animals that absorbs oxygen from the water

habitat the kind of place in which an animal lives

host a living plant or animal in or on which a parasite lives

invertebrate an animals without a backbone

krill small, shrimplike animals that live in oceans throughout the world

larva the immature form of certain animals, which differs from the adult form in many ways; crustaceans, fish, insects, and mollusks typically have a larval stage

mammal an animal that feeds its young on the mother's milk

mollusk a group of soft-bodied animals that have no bones, including snails, slugs, clams, mussels, oysters, squids, octopuses, and scallops

molt to shed feathers, skin, hair, shell, antlers, or other growths before a new growth

mutualism a relationship between two creatures in which both benefit

organism a living thing

parasite a living thing that feeds off another living thing called a host

pectoral of, in, or on the breast or chest

pinnae ear flaps (singular is pinna)

plankton the mass of tiny living things that drift with the current at or near the surface of oceans, lakes, and other bodies of water

pod a group of dolphins, whales, or seals

predator an animal that preys upon other animals

radula a horny band in the mouth of a mollusk set with hard teeth

reptile an animal that has dry, scaly skin and breathes with lungs

school a group of fish or water animals swimming together

siphon a tube-shaped organ of a clam, oyster, or certain other shellfish for drawing in and expelling water

sonar an artificial system that uses sound energy to locate objects underwater; submarines typically use sonar to collect information about their surroundings

spawn to release eggs in water for fertilization

species a kind of living thing; members of a species share many characteristics and are able to interbreed

symbiosis a relationship between two creatures in which at least one of them benefits

tubercle a small, rounded swelling or knob on an animal or plant

venom a poisonous substance produced by many kinds of animals to injure, kill, or digest prey

vertebrate an animal with a spinal column (backbone) and a cranium (brain case)

wean to accustom a young animal to food other than its mother's milk

Resources

Books

Journey Under the Sea by Linda M. Pitkin
(Oxford University Press, 2003)
Travel into the hidden world of the ocean with this book,
which includes color photographs of ocean habitats and
the creatures who live in them.

Oceans by Seymour Simon (Smithsonian, 2006)
Explore our beautiful, fragile oceans and their
many ecosystems in this book.

The Deep-Sea Floor by Sneed B. Collard and Gregory C.
Wenzel (Charlesbridge, 2003)
This volume explores the weird and wonderful animal life
that lives in the deepest parts of the oceans.

Websites

Monterey Bay Aquarium Animal Guide
http://www.montereybayaquarium.org
An interactive animal guide lets you explore whole
categories of ocean animals or look for a particular
favorite.

Planet Ocean Learning Adventures
http://school.discoveryeducation.com/schooladventures/
planetocean/ocean.html
Fun facts about the ocean and some of its fascinating
inhabitants can be found at this site from Discovery
Education.

SeaWorld: Aquatic Seafari
http://www.seaworld.org/wild-world/safari/
virtual-aquarium
This virtual aquarium is an interactive guide to such
unique sea animals as coral and sea stars.

Acknowledgments

Cover photograph: SuperStock (Science Faction)

Illustrations: © Art-Tech

Photographs:

Alamy: 19 (B. M. Uz)

Dreamstime: 7 (P. Mitov), 9 (Nanisub), 15 (J. Anderson),
19 (N. Smit), 21 (M. Blajenov), 35 (D. van der Linden),
40 (Z. Kizilkaya), 42 (P. Mitov), 45 (F. Mun Kwan)

FLPA: 8 (Flip Nicklin), 23 (N. Wu), 26 (D. P.Wilson),
27 (C. Newbert), 28 (Frans Lanting), 30 (D. Larsen),
33 (Flip Nicklin), 34 (FotoNatura), 39 (S. Jonasson),
37 (D. Duckett)

Fotolia: 29 (Iofoto), 43 (F. Steinberg)

iStock Photo: 6 (Dennis Sabo), 16 (A. Koen),
18 (C. Lukhaup)

Photolibrary: 10 (R. Herrmann), 12 (G. Holland)

Photos.com: 11, 13, 14, 17, 22, 24, 25, 31, 32, 36,
38, 41, 44

Index